MW01068366

THE ART OF
THE BRIEF

Become a Subject Matter Expert

SPENCER BEATTY

The Art of the Brief

Copyright © 2018 by Mentor Enterprises

All rights reserved. No part of this book may be reproduced or transmitted in any form or by any means without written permission from Mentor Enterprises, Inc.

Printed in USA by Mentor Enterprises Inc.

PUBLISHED BY
MENTOR®
ENTERPRISES, INC.

123 Castle Dr. STE C, Madison, AL 35758

256.830.8282

info@mentorinc.us

1st Edition

ISBN-13: 978-1-940370-20-0

The views expressed in this book are those of the author and do not reflect the official policy or position of the United States Army, Defense Department, or the United States Government.

Contents

PART SEVEN: REVISITING STAGE FRIGHT 171

PART EIGHT: ADVANCED TOPICS 175

PART NINE: LISTS 189

Updates and Corrections are available online at:
http://www.asktop.net/aob1ed
Access Code: BEAAOB18

GUIDEPOSTS YOU WILL FIND THROUGHOUT THIS BOOK

BE YOURSELF

"You wouldn't worry so much about what others think of you if your realized how seldom they do"—Eleanor Roosevelt

The nature of briefing flushes the acting instinct in everyone. This is good. Yet, trying to come across as something more or something less than the real you will never resonate with an audience.

EXPECTATION MANAGEMENT

Briefing is a balance of information and emotion. You must prepare and execute your briefing and in the process, you are putting yourself in the spotlight. Expectation management is a powerful tool for streamlining preparation, presentation, and keeping calm.

RESEARCH ALWAYS PAYS

Style or substance? Yes. You need to have the ability to hold your audience's attention. However, a paper-thin veneer of expertise will become obvious at the first sign of inquiry or disruption. There is simply no substitute for knowing your subject, yourself, your audience, and your venue.

CLASSROOM MANAGEMENT

There are audiences that are completely attentive and respectful, but you are better off recognizing that there will be at least one problem child wherever you go. It's rarely personal, but requires an effective, professional response.

ART OF PERSUASION

A professional demeanor that keeps the audience's attention is a must, but so is the art of persuasion. No matter how routine your information is, there is at least one thing you would like your audience to think about

1

PART ONE: "WHO"

"A good teacher, like a good entertainer, first must hold his audience's attention; then he can teach a lesson."

—*John Henrik Clarke*

"WHO" FAQ'S

1. How do I make a presentation that speaks to the audience?

   a. Don't just create a presentation for yourself.

   b. Avoid the temptation to take a one size fits all approach. See "It's About Communication" (Page "It's About Communication (Speak Their Language)" on page 7)

2. Is there a way to appeal to everyone when there are so many personality types?

   a. Being yourself and knowing your material are the surest ways to appeal to a wide range of people.

   b. Becoming familiar with personality types and preparing to engage different learning styles requires research and rehearsal *See "A Word About Personality Types" (Page 14)*

3. How do I deal with sharpshooters and hecklers?

    a. Present an emotionally flat response and do not take it personal

    b. Respond patiently, professionally, and realize that the audience probably appreciates the heckler as much as you do.

    c. Maintain a sense of humor

    d. Redirect comments forward, "That is actually addressed in a few slides." Or, "I left room to go into those issues at the end." See "A Word About Personality Types" *(Page 14) and "Audience Types" (Page 27)*

4. I normally brief my co-workers, but now I have to take a presentation to a different organization as a guest presenter. How can I best prepare?

    a. Expect the disadvantages of not knowing the ropes or the inherent power structures and personalities. However, you can also expect grace as a guest. Appreciate the freedom of having no baggage or built in friction.

    b. You biggest challenge will be all the things you take for granted i.e. Projectors, Microphones, Podiums, Markers, Pointers, Computer systems, etc. Plan to coordinate early and often with your point of contact.
See "Audience Types" (Page 27)

5. The Audience for my next presentation will have a large variety of people. What should I look for or change in my presentation?

    a. You need to make the safest version of your brief that you can. Depending on the topic and the age of the youngest audience members, you may need to alter quite a few things. Most importantly, remove anything that piques political or religious sentiments or words that seem loaded in today's world.

b. Be yourself and direct everything in the direction of mutual goals. You have been dealing with countless personalities your whole life, hence, you can follow your instincts to a large degree.

See "A Word About Personality Types" (Page 14)

IT'S NOT ABOUT YOU

Tell Me About an Important Day in Your Life

Perhaps you've been unfortunate enough to hear that question during an interview or simply covered the topic during a friendly conversation. In any case, what came to mind? Hang on to that for a moment. You may have asked a question in return.

Who wants to know?

THAT is the right question.

Now, go back to the first memory that came to mind and put it in the context of a job interview. Do you change your story? Perhaps you should focus on a day you made an important decision. Maybe you should talk about a time when you realized you had a passion for something related to the focus of this company. Perhaps you should take the easy route and just talk about how you met your significant other.

In any case, the big disadvantage you have in that situation is the fact that you do not necessarily know why they are asking or how important the question is.

On the other hand, the interview may be an extension of the organization and its hiring practices, but at the end of the day, you need to leave the right impression on this one person who is asking the question. Are they young or old? Upbeat or sullen? Uptight or casual? Do they have pictures of their pets in the office? What about a prized possession like a car? Instinctively, you will try to tailor an answer that could connect with this person that you have only a few clues about, but that is the point. Your answer will vary because of your audience.

What if it was a drill sergeant who asked you that question on the first day of basic training? What situation did you find yourself in to have that happen? Chances are, your drill sergeant has both a flair for the dramatic and a sick sense of humor. Chances are also that everyone else is watching and ever so thankful they aren't you. Now that's complicated. But not really, because there won't be a good answer. Stop trying to think of one and get whatever happens next over with quickly.

Try the following question out with the below audiences.

"What happens during an Eclipse?"

- Your niece/nephew
- A classroom of 5th Graders
- Your Physical Science teacher

You could answer such a question in a moment with a few animated phrases and hand/arm gestures, or provide several pages of technical phrases and equations. There are vast differences between talking to one person and a group, age groups, education levels, personal relations and formal relations, etc.

Don't worry about it though. As a human being, you are intuitively good at adapting what you say and how you say it. However, if you put anything in the context of public speaking or a "spotlight," then all bets are off.

Even if you are comfortable on center stage and have a natural gift with people (which would put you in a very small portion of the population), then consider that throwing a ball may come very naturally, but pitching an 80-mph fastball can only come with knowledge and training. A successful presentation will hinge on the degree to which the briefer made some careful calculations about the audience.

This chapter will take a detailed look at specific audience types and the sorts of individuals you can find out there as well as common mistakes to avoid.

It's Not About You... Because it is.

You want to come across well. You want to persuade. You want to be understood. You want to make a good impression.

It all sounds very self-centered, but it also seems very natural. Your audience matters because YOU matter. It's hard to just stumble on the ever desired attributes of self-respect, dignity, and opportunity. You will spend a lifetime building these qualities...one audience at a time. Ironically, you will build more quickly if you think of others more than yourself, especially when you communicate. Have you ever heard this quote?

> "People don't care how much you know until they know how much you care."

The quote is often attributed to Theodore Roosevelt and given recent fame by motivational speaker, Zig Ziglar. Aside from being catchy and proverbial, the saying usually resonates because we all remember brilliant people who left little impact on our lives because of their disregard for us and others.

The military version of that quote might sound familiar as well.

"Respect is a two-way street."

 Everyone has seen the difference between earned respect and obligatory respect. It is likely that caring about people and the organization made the difference.

This book will not suggest that you turn into a sensitivity guru or motivational speaker during your presentations because there are many more practical ways to demonstrate you care.

Let's turn the tables for a moment and think about what an audience who cares about you or your content will do during your presentation. What do you want to see when you look out across the audience? What sorts of expressions would you like to see on their faces?

If you are lucky, they are showing signs of active listening.

- Focused on you and not their phones or notes
- Generally maintaining eye contact
- Nodding, smiling, or looking inquisitive when appropriate
- Provide answers to questions that you insert into the presentation
- Etc.

Is all this positive energy for real or an act? Ever been a great 'active listener' for a boss whose every word was nonsense as far as you were concerned? For this discussion, it doesn't matter. What matters is why people extend these courtesies. It is because there is always more future potential for someone who cares. At some point, everyone needs the benefit of the doubt from their peers or the attention of everyone in the room. People who are uncaring or discourteous listeners often find that retribution awaits.

The flip side of active listening is effective communication. An excellent communicator rarely makes anyone "fake" the signs of active listening. If nothing else, you should speak their language. It is always better to gain genuine enthusiasm. Like respect, such enthusiasm is earned and easy to accomplish with some effort and dedication.

It's About Communication (Speak Their Language)

Since you obviously want your audience to be engaged as opposed to just obligingly polite, you need to speak their language. Depending on the audience this will require either a little or a lot of research. No matter how ingrained you are in the audience you will never be completely free from the need to research, and what is more, you may need to adjust your language all the way up to and during "show time." When you speak the language, it not only shows that you care about them as an organization and as individuals, but it shows that you care enough to listen.

Your two greatest temptations will be:

1. To create a briefing that would inform and convince you of certain facts and possibilities.

2. To create a briefing that would wow a general audience without any real tailoring to the local audience (Think of training teams and product representatives).

7

The briefing that convinces you...but not your audience.

Situation: You want to revitalize a leaders' sports day on the training calendar, but the commander has been dismissive of the idea. You are granted a short office call to make a case for the program and there are many leaders in the organization that are in favor of the program's return.

The program went away after a football game resulted in two serious injuries that ended one leader's career and embarrassed the command. That was a while ago and, even after several changes of command, there is still an abiding sense of unnecessary risk associated with bringing back leaders' sports day.

Desk-side Briefing: After some thought, you prepare your talking points and present them to the commander. You emphasize how many units have a similar program and conduct them without any safety issues or significant injuries. You volunteer to research the best implementation and put together a risk assessment for each event. You then indicate how important it could be for team building and then indicate that there is widespread support for the program in the unit.

Result: The commander did not need a reminder about how popular the idea is. It seems like that's all they've heard about lately. (This may have only been a concluding statement on your part, but remember, the last thing you say tends to overshadow prior content and guide the conversation.) The commander reminds you that the previous program was noted for meticulous risk assessments and they didn't prevent the problem. In conclusion, you hear that competitiveness and varying degrees of athletic ability come together in ways that really can't be controlled. The unit's PT Scores and FTX results indicate that the unit is on a good path and there's no reason to invite negative attention on an otherwise great unit.

ART OF PERSUASION

Better Approach: You comb through recent talking points from the Army Chief of Staff and tailor your statements to fit into those priorities that the Chain of Command is certainly tracking. You research the biographies of the Brigade Commander and Commanding General and discover that their prior units had similar programs which they participated in. What is more, the Commanding General's Command Philosophy emphasizes that the army "is a physical sport" and that Soldiers and leaders need physical challenges and novelty. To top it off, he was the Quarterback on the West Point team. You then package these salient points into a few simple phrases and conclude your talking points with the bit about the CG being a Quarterback.

Result: The commander listens carefully, makes few facial expressions but nods a few times and seems contemplative. "Okay," you hear. "I'll run it by the boss and see what I can do. Thanks!" It is likely you will have a leader's sports program shortly.

Of course, you can rarely hope on finding such a wealth of supporting facts from your research, but if you don't know a few specific things about what and who drives the decision-making with your audience, then you will usually come across as irrelevant or lackluster. Research always pays.

It will seem as if you don't care.

Too often, an individual or staff will focus too much on the language of the audience or commander. Yes, there really can be 'too much of a good thing.' People are somewhat attuned to anyone that is, to be frank, 'blowing smoke up their backside.' You can call it 'sucking up' or 'brown nosing' or what have you.

In any case, it is usually transparent, especially in the context of a persuasive briefing or sales pitch. Nothing turns people off quite like manipulative language. Maybe you've noticed that a good car salesperson asks you a few things about yourself, your family, your interests, and then, little by little, associate the vehicle's attributes with your lifestyle. Ever had one overdo it? Exactly, don't be that person.

The briefing that would wow a general audience, but...

In the Army, decisions often result in committing time, unit funds, or both towards a particular end. Since time and money are usually in short supply, a decision brief can take on the tone of a sales pitch. This is when the language becomes generalized and weighted to the "upside" of a proposition.

Situation: You attended a Department of Defense seminar which introduced you to a new piece of technology that you believe would solve some of the communication issues your unit encounters in the field. You were asked to back brief the commander and staff on any products that may be worth pursuing. You paid close attention to the product representatives and practically memorized their selling points. You collected flyers, pamphlets, and business cards as the foundation of your presentation to the unit. It seems easy, the company in question clearly spent thousands of dollars to put together good-looking promotional materials and obviously know how to craft their talking points to get units to invest in their products. You figure all you must do is condense the best of the bunch and you will be good

Result: Before you are even halfway through your presentation you start to get some questions you didn't expect and aren't sure how to answer. When it is over, it seems clear that no one is interested in the product that you legitimately thought would help out. Ironically, the signal experts in your unit acknowledged that this product would indeed solve the issues that emerged during the last FTX, but there would be a trade-off for other problems. You have a hunch that the second set of issues aren't nearly as bad as people now think, but it is too late. You go home believing that the unit may have missed an opportunity to do better in the future for a reasonable cost.

Your presentation could wow a general audience, like the one you found yourself in at the recent conference. It even proposed solutions to problems that were unit specific, but it did not look at other unit specific concerns. This is where you might learn that the more people a presentation appeals to, the less meaningful it is.

ART OF PERSUASION
Better Approach: You look at the material but realize that those business cards provided you with a point of contact for any questions. Instead of trying to "wow" the team with an innovative product and some well-crafted selling points, you decide to get ahead of potential friction. You spend some time with the folks in your commo shop and learn early on what you were bound to learn later (while in the spotlight). You grab the most cynical member of your team and contact the company for a conference call. You discover that the proposed solution will leave a couple of new problems for the unit to figure out, but they are small potatoes compared to the advantages. What's more important is that you are ready for tough questions and you aligned a potential critic to your team before show-time.

Result: The commander asks you to get the answers to a few more questions and requests a meeting with a field representative who can bring the product in for hands-on examination. You believe that the chances of the unit adopting the product are 50/50 at best. However, you sense that your commander and peers respect your approach to solving problems. Even if the proposal fails, you will likely be held in higher regard because of your well-prepared presentation.

This isn't a case of ordinary 'friction' (i.e., resistance) short-circuiting a briefing. This is a case of specific friction. The original sales pitch was designed to address general resistance to purchasing the product, but your organization has specific concerns. Those concerns, like specific motivators, are all that matters. You aren't speaking the language of your audience if you don't know what their specific concerns will be. If you only try to gloss over this type of resistance with more positive slogans, your audience will see you as cavalier. They will perceive that you don't care.

Think about the unique language of military culture. If you are serving your country, you know that your civilian friends and family understand some of the things you say just as well as most people understand two physicists talking about Dark Matter. The same can be said of many service members who retire and experience the civilian language barrier.

But that is just the beginning. Even amongst those who share the common language of army acronyms, slogans, inside jokes, and phrases know the differences between the language of an Airborne (Airborne!!!) unit and an Armor Unit, Ranger Unit, SOCOM unit, Sustainment Unit, etc. If you were to present information to all these units during a month, then hopefully no two presentations would be exactly alike.

:) **BE YOURSELF**
Under no circumstances should you pretend to be a part of something that you are not. Is there anything more embarrassing than someone trying to act like an insider when they are new or an outsider. There are countless comedy skits and premises built on the awkwardness of that situation. The idea is not to imitate or act the part of a local but to conduct enough research that you know what drives the local culture and economy. Speak to the motivators and concerns of your audience. That's what people who care do. At the very least, they will know you cared enough to do your research.

Another temptation that many people encounter when they are supposed to conduct a briefing or presentation is the temptation to "sound smart." If you are like most people you have a vocabulary of roughly 15,000 words, however, you only need about 4000 of those words to carry on meaningful discussions, laugh at your favorite sitcoms, and understand the daily news feed. Everyone knows that "smart people" use big words or uncommon words in casual conversations. This might be true, but when you are only playing the part by loading "smart" words and phrases into your presentation, it will show. People are very good at picking up on subtle clues in their environment and trying to use language that is not natural to you will always resonate.

 If you want to be smart, then just know your stuff. A confident, simple presentation with real depth behind the talking points will always go further than a smoke-screen of fancy words and phrases. The only thing people dislike more than incompetence is insincerity and pretense.

Tailoring your message shouldn't be rocket science. Most units, and organizations wear their values and culture on their sleeve. Everything from SOPs, to posters, to the way people wear their hair and clothing, etc. will signal the sorts of talking points that might gain traction vs. those that will turn people away. You are not trying to become a native, only understand what makes them tick. If you know that, then you can use your own language to speak to theirs.

"They may forget what you said, but they will never forget how you made them feel."—Carl W. Buechner

A Word About Personality Types

The movie screen flickers a funny segment to a broad audience on a Saturday night. There are chuckles, belly laughs, and everything in between. Then, there is that occasional person who looks either angry or, surprisingly, looks heartbroken. It doesn't make sense unless you are that person.

Who knows what images may have provoked personal experience, values, or tragic losses in their past on the screen. The writer, director, and actors did everything to make the audience laugh, but you can never get the entire audience on board. People are complicated, and ultimately, everyone is a culture unto themselves.

Similarly, even the most expertly prepared and presented briefing cannot guarantee a positive or even logical reception. There are always factors regarding your audience for which you cannot prepare or control. However, you may be able to reduce communication failures if you take some time to recognize and respect different personality types and the way in which they prefer to receive information.

As an example of how this works, if you were approached by a guest speaker who wanted to brief your supervisor about a new technology and they asked you what "the boss" likes, dislikes, and focuses on during briefings, what would you say? Your answer is rooted the traits of your supervisor's personality type and leadership style. The leadership and professional culture that you work with is, inadvertently, training you to present information in a certain way. When you change environments or leaders, you can expect a shock in how a "perfect" briefing is received.

:) **BE YOURSELF**

How can you fix this? It is impossible to have the kind of "intel" you need to be successful in different briefing environments for different audiences. The simple answer is to go in with a sense of flexibility. Keep the core of your presentation (the bottom line information, facts, and advantages/disadvantages, etc.) and be ready to rearrange the priority and emphasis of your talking points according to how you're are being received.

It may sound complicated, or akin to preparing several briefings, but you make these sorts of shifts instinctively in most social and professional settings. How many times have you begun a conversation with one tone and agenda and then finished with something entirely different? As long as you know your material and don't use your format or presentation as a crutch or anchor, you may be surprised how easy it is to move your agenda like a chameleon into whatever situation you find yourself.

What are the personality types?

The question is not as straightforward as "how many chromosomes do people have?" The very idea of personality "types" is subjective, and there are various approaches. You might have taken a personality test or two in your life and then received either a four-letter acronym, color, animal, adjective, or other, that best described your type. Each of these methods, and many more, are useful as one tool in a larger kit bag.

Most tests and teachings are the intellectual property of those researchers that created them, and a detailed program that teaches you how to utilize personality types to your advantage will require a fiscal commitment. It is probably worth the investment in yourself to go into depth with one of the programs at some point. But, it might be a little easier to just pull from your current environment. You, your peers, your friends, your boss, your family, etc. are all unique individuals with unique personalities that fit roughly into various "types."

Chances are you will begin your preparation for your any briefing with an approach that would appeal to you. There's nothing wrong with that because there are other people who see the world the way you do and if something is not good enough for your standards, then why would you sell it to someone else? But, in accordance with prior warnings within this book. Do not think that this is the ideal solution. Now, as you finalize your presentation, keep your research and notes handy and then lift and shift your focus.

Worst Case Personality

Who is the last person that you would want to brief with this material, or ever? Now, if you had to do exactly that, what would you do? How would you change the presentation? What facts would you dig up in addition to what you already have? What part of the topic would you spend the most time on? What types of sentences, tone, and body language would you use?

It is unlikely that this person will show up, unless of course this just happens to be the reality you live in at this phase of your career, but a part of your brief may bring out similar qualities in a member of your audience. If you are ready for the worst and could shift to a "hidden-slide" or separate page of references on a moment's notice, then you are practically ready for anything.

CLASSROOM MANAGEMENT
Remember, always consider 'your plan' as a base-line. Once you "SP," flexibility and adaptiveness are the name of the game. Just as with an Operations Order, the specific plan might be meaningless once the wheels hit the road, but the basic facts and estimates remain as a foundation for command decisions.

You are not going into a briefing to execute a precise course of action, but to meet a certain intent. You are in charge, and _you_ decide how to adjust fire during the engagement.

The Rabbit Trailer

There will usually be a 'creative type' or two in the room. They may even be the most important person in the room. For the most part, interacting with this type of personality is pleasant, or at least not intimidating. They often crack positive or witty jokes and find new ideas and information genuinely fascinating. They will usually encourage more dialogue, not less, and can see concepts as if they were already complete.

Wow, what a great person to have in the room, right? Don't count on it.

The downside of such a personality type is that they can't help but daydream and start the gears turning when information is on the table. While you are preparing a transition to the next major topic, they are ready to build a franchise on the current concept and want to dive into all the possibilities. They will throw an otherwise innocent and complementary question into the presentation and divert the entire audience into a rabbit trail. After all, these are the personalities with the gift of inspiring others' imaginations as well. Not exactly what you are looking for when the inspiration is driving the audience away from your presentation.

It might be simple human nature, but any topic other than the one we all sat down to discuss seems to be a fascinating one at any given time. How many training meetings have turned into an NCOER professional development session? Ever been to the steering committee that turned into a sensing session?

In any case, the creative types will be both your best friend and worst enemy depending on the situation. The simple answer is just to expect it. It is not an insult, or an inconvenience as much as it is just part of the game. If you take it personally or seem flustered by the diversion, it will show and shift the tone of the room away from embracing you and hence, your briefing.

 CLASSROOM MANAGEMENT
You have seen other speakers use redirecting cues, so just rehearse a couple and be ready to use them... Calmly, patiently, and professionally.

"And that...is precisely the direction I would like to see this discussion go, and the last couple of slides cover that question..."

"Excellent comment, that is something we get into during/when..."

"Interesting. I think we'll be able to explore that near the end, but the next couple of charts will help clarify."

Since your rabbit-trailer may have some, or much, authority in the room the idea is never to imply that 'we don't have time for that,' or 'sure, maybe later,' but to imply that the upcoming portion of the brief is exactly what this person wants to see. Even if it is only partially correct, you are projecting their imagination forward in expectancy instead of into the present where it will spiral out of control.

Think of such moments as an opportunity to enhance anticipation for the rest of the brief as opposed to a detractor.

The Empath

Another common personality type you will find in almost any setting is the individual who seems hardwired for compassion and empathy. Once again, that is a fantastic person to have in your life and beneficial to almost any group. What is more, this is the person who will usually shift their energy to supporting you in any way they can if you seem to be stumbling, losing the crowd, or otherwise need some assistance. For the most part, there aren't a lot of disadvantages to this personality.

But are you communicating to them?

You aren't there to be supported or assisted. You are there to assist, inform, and in some way, support the group's mission. Therefore, you must communicate. If you tend to be empathetic in nature, then your briefing is already taking the shape of one that will appeal to others like you. But maybe you are most driven by "hard facts," and believe you need to keep emotion out of it.

That may sound like the best professional approach, but organizations are made of real lives that are impacted by logical, calculated decisions. The empathic view, while more concerned with 'soft dynamics' can be the most important and often forgotten dynamic.

 If you have presented an audit-proof trail of percentages, facts, statistics, and a logical sequence of events, then you have done well. But your presentation will fall flat on your audience to some degree. What is the human aspect of your topic? How does this impact people? What are the second and third order effects on the organization?

Even cold and calculating leaders care about the future of the organization and perception. Leaders are, necessarily, all too aware of how important the human element is, even if they get blindsided by it after a decision is made. Help them get in front of it and understand these elements ahead of time.

A brief that interweaves empathetic appeal leaves the impression that you care, draws people in on a deeper level, and even makes logic driven personalities want to thank you for the 'insight.'

The Hard Charger

Welcome to the real world. It's no secret that successful people in the both the military and business often have a hard charger personality type. People who fit most naturally into this personality type are cut from the same cloth as notable folks like Tom Brady, Patton, Steve Jobs, Political Frontrunners, etc. Even those who are not inclined this way discover that the culture of the workplace flushes out those attributes.

The bottom line is, does your presentation focus on winning?

When an organization becomes more efficient, more effective, or more appealing to those outside of it, then winning may be implied. However, the fact that this 'helps us win' should be literally stated during the presentation. That does not mean to be a 'cheesy' or 'motivational speaker' about the idea, but your talking points should edge toward the literal idea of winning.

Hard chargers want to move the organization down the field and take the goal post. In fact, a real hard charger wants to rip the goal post out of the turf and stake it through the chest of the opposition. However, even the more timid souls among us do not wake up every day with hopes of "sucking at life."

A common question to many presenters is "what's the 'so what'?" Or, in other words, this is great information and those are excellent points but why do we care? If the 'so what' is 'we win,' then right or wrong it will have appeal and keep their attention. Yes, everyone has seen individuals and organizations that focus so much on winning that they overlook the big picture and fall into disaster, but if your presentation is worthwhile, then you there's no issue with presenting it as such.

If nothing else, keep that 'this is a win' mentality in your tone and body language. If you take on the aura of a coach who is leading the group to a victory on the field then all the better.

CLASSROOM MANAGEMENT

The Hard Charger will have no qualms about interrupting you at any time, with any critique; even when you are mid-sentence. If you sense the signature assertiveness of a hard charger and if they are one of the senior members of the audience it is best to embrace the interruption and provide a concise answer. This is in opposition to the, "Excellent question, we will get to that in a few slides..." approach. This is the moment when you will be glad that you know your stuff. See it as an opportunity to demonstrate you are cool under pressure and ready to change gears on a moment's notice. If you eagerly cue a certain slide from later in the deck to facilitate the answer, the Hard Charger will likely see that, while they want answers and they want a presenter that can handle themselves, they usually do not want to disrupt the agenda. Confidently show respect to the command personality and you will likely regain the initiative.

There's a reason you see the word "win" in advertising on an almost daily basis.

Your bottom line up front, no matter how you phrase it, should communicate "this helps you win."

The Networker

Networking is the key to success in practically every endeavor. Most people instinctively utilize the networks and human resources available to them, but a natural networker instinctively strengthens, builds, expands, and exploits networks. When a networker sees a briefing or interacts with people in general, they are looking for new doors, alliances, and human resources. They do not see success in an organization as something that can be found in a vacuum or on an island.

Some ideas and changes to an organization can have the effect of introverting the way business is done. Sometimes, an over competitive spirit leads business practices to exclude outside influences or resources. On the other hand, just exploiting resources in the networks can be a negative tendency as well.

In any case, if you want to make sure you appeal to the networker or just the networker in everyone, you should look at your talking points and consider if this perspective is relevant or if there are such implications. You might only add or enhance one such talking point but the immediate interest it would generate, or the likelihood of approval, might increase exponentially.

People want to know how they affect the world around them. If you can, let them know how your proposal contributes. It implies you care and demonstrates that you "get it."

The 'So What'

The big takeaway is remembering that your communication style and personality type will drive your initial plans and preparation. You can't help but put your view of what right looks like into the product. This is the best place to start, but before you are complete, you must recognize that preparing to meet the needs of the audience is what leads to success.

Levels of Education and Technical Expertise

There are very homogenous organizations in which most members share a similar level of education and share similar technical expertise. These are few and far between. Most audiences range from 'street smarts' to PhDs, and the organization requires both technical and administrative skill sets. This doesn't mean you can judge a book by its cover because often there are folks with advanced degrees working in jobs that don't necessarily require them.

The lesson here is that you should not make assumptions about your audience based on what they do, their age, or the primary mission of the organization. What matters most is recognizing your own limitations and strengths regarding education and technical understanding.

BE YOURSELF

Ultimately, it doesn't matter where you fall in the spectrum so long as you recognize what you are trying to say and who you are saying it too. However, the worst thing you can do is to try and 'sound smart' as opposed to just sounding like yourself. This book will cover aspects of overcoming stage fright in a later chapter, but the more comfortable you are in your skin, the better off you are (which is true in general).

This topic was touched on earlier, but it bears repeating.

Planning to insert "thousand-dollar words" or technical jargon into your brief for no reason other than to sound smart is a sure loser. Not because people don't appreciate a good grasp of language and technology, but it is easy to spot someone who is speaking above their comfort level. The result is an audience that feels awkward or slightly embarrassed about the presentation.

RESEARCH ALWAYS PAYS

It is not unusual to find yourself in over your head with either the topic or the audience. This may be uncomfortable, but it is okay to present the material from where you are in language that is natural for you. Most communication from small talk, to television, to the internet, is conducted on a level well below graduate school textbooks and no one considers it a problem. Ultimately, most people want plain, clear, and concise information that they can utilize for their purposes.

Seek out technical advice and run your presentation through someone you consider to be a technical expert if you are uncertain. Just remember what the intent of your brief is and concern yourself with the most efficient and direct way to accomplish that intent. Using heady language or terminology rarely does the trick. If such language and terminology is a must, then study it and read about it until it does feel natural. After all, everything you now know was new and unfamiliar at one point.

The Flip Side

The flip side of education and expertise is the risk of sounding conde-scending or patronizing. When someone attempts to diminish another person by inserting complex language or topics into a conversation, it is all too transparent to anyone nearby. Sometimes, it is not intentional, but the effect is the same.

Ultimately, language is not only powerful but can drive a wedge between people. Your goal is always to empower the topic and avoid any gaps between you and your audience.

The key, as always, is just to be yourself. Per-haps you are more educated and use a lot of big words that your audience avoids in daily conversations. So what? Is that how you are? Then it will work.

Consider this. You have seen at least one sitcom in which a person is trying to sound smarter than they were turned into comedy gold. How-ever, haven't you seen something just as embarrassing/hilarious when a smart person tries to fit in with a new group by attempting to talk with slang and hip phrases. When someone is out of their element, it shows.

If anything is more condescending than talking down to someone it is trying to talk "dumber" to sound "normal." The audience has an intuitive sense that they are somehow being made fun of or that the speaker is inadvertently turning them into a caricature.

Think of it this way. Every first-grade teacher has a greater command of the English language than their students. However, there is a dif-ference between a teacher who simply uses complex language in a normal and natural way such that it becomes a part of the pupil's lives and one who uses language to make sure the students feel ignorant. The first teacher is just themselves. The second one is making a point.

BE YOURSELF

If, for some reason, you think you may come across as 'too smart,' just realize that people rarely complain about an instructor or presenter who was too qualified,' 'too knowledgeable,' or 'too articulate.' On the other hand, a briefer who is condescending is rated lower than one who is ignorant.

The one litmus test to know if you may be leaning toward showing the worst side of yourself in the language you choose is in your mood. When people are on the defense or have a grudge, the negative aspects of speech naturally boil up to the mouth. No matter what happens during a briefing, if you find your defenses are up or that you take issue with a comment or person, then KNOW that the audience can read this on you. Your body language is in the spotlight and unmistakable.

Stop, take a breath, and treat everyone in that room as you would any high-ranking individual. Biting your tongue and checking your attitude are daily professional skills.

Don't confuse the physical posture of controlling a room during a presentation with being the boss...unless, of course; you are the boss. Then, just remember that respect is always the best plan. Heat from the top always burns deeper.

AUDIENCE TYPES

Now that there has been some discussion about personality types, language and the focus of your presentation, it is time to look specifically at different audiences in the collective sense. There is a big difference between briefing an individual and briefing an auditorium. Likewise, you would want to know if your audience was composed of your peers or high-ranking people. The variety and complexity of audience composition is almost without limits. However, here are a few main types of audiences you will likely encounter during your career.

Audience 1: Your Organization

In sports, it is usually a good thing to play on your turf or the home-field advantage as they say. You should feel more comfortable conducting a brief within familiar territory and among people that you spend 40 or more hours a week interacting with.

On the home field you can set the conditions, directly impact the physical preparations, and if anything goes wrong during the event, you can access your work area and know where everything is stored and how to turn on/off the lights. You can conduct rehearsals at your leisure, don't have to worry that you left something "back at the office" and won't lose any time or assume any risk getting from Point A to Point B.

Another advantage is that you know who is who, you understand the formal and informal power structure. You know the personality types and are fluent in the various communication styles. You figure out what drives the decision-making process and the ins and outs of talking to the decision makers. What is more, you know what types of visuals (or lack thereof) that go best and probably created some percentage of the everyday briefing products.

EXPECTATION MANAGEMENT

Before you take this audience for granted, just realize that there is a flip side to everything. Doubtless, the home field is where you will likely conduct most of the briefings in your career. If you work in sales or training, then the opposite is probably true. In any case, there are unique disadvantages that go with briefing your organization.

You have relationships with everyone in your organization which means that any baggage or grudges between you and anyone else will enter the briefing room with you. Also, no one in the audience has any illusions about who you are, what you know, and your general level of experience. All of these things can have advantages, but there is bound to be subtext and static between you and your message with more a than a few folks in the room.

No big deal. You will navigate these obstacles and hazards the same way you do every day because this is where you practically live.

It is a jungle, but it is your jungle. So here are the big cautions:

Allowing questions or comments to go from zero to personal in one second:

While Captain X-Ray may routinely be a thorn in your flesh, that doesn't mean his question or comment about your last statement should register on a personal level. Sure, it may be just another opportunity to mess with you, but if you 'go there' the rest of your briefing will be downhill in one way or another. Just respond to the comment or question with a transitional response that you practiced ahead of time or reference to appropriate supporting material for more information.

After all, everyone knows if you have baggage with someone and will be waiting to see how you handle yourself. What is more, audience members are also on the spot. No one appreciates unnecessary interruptions, bullying, or obvious inattentiveness. If you handle yourself well, then you will walk away with tremendous respect for it, and it could even come at a heckler's expense.

Being Too Casual:

The rigid rank structure of the military creates a formality and decorum that is rarely exceeded in the civilian sector. That being said, different organizations have varying levels of formality in their daily operations. This could be an aspect of command climate, lax discipline, or it could be the nature of the organization's primary mission and daily routine. In any case, you might be more comfortable with the ranking individual on the home team than you are with the lowest ranking members of other organizations.

There is a high probability that you have worked closely with the boss on several things and even shared jokes, cultural memes, and family events. Once you are assigned a briefing, do not take anything for granted or act like someone has your back, or are willing to accept something subpar just because they know you. What's more, do not think you have a license to be overly funny, or make light of any shortcomings during the brief. Your peers and supervisor have your back, but you must earn your place at the table every day.

None the less, the appropriate use of inside jokes, references to common goals/struggles, and previous victories give you credibility and brings everyone in on an emotional and psychological level that a guest speaker could never accomplish. Review your materials and talking points and adjust for greatest effect.

Audience 2: Unfamiliar Territory

Then there is the opposite situation. Maybe you've had that email show up in your inbox or that phone call that informs you about a briefing you need to give tomorrow at some headquarters you've never visited before. Or perhaps you spend a lot of time on TDY and it is always something different. Anxiety is often the gut reaction to the situation, but there are blessings within this context as well.

When you conduct a briefing in an unfamiliar setting to an audience of strangers you are at the ultimate audience disadvantage. Aside from simply preparing information and backup charts for a variety of situations, you will know nothing about the command climate, leadership styles, communication styles, etc. that will contribute to the way you and your presentation are perceived.

Perhaps you put a slide up on the screen or simply hand out a 'placemat' to the team, and you immediately get a sour look or two from the ranking people in the room. You don't know what it is about your product that hit them wrong, but it was something. You can't help but wonder what else you are about to step into as the briefing proceeds.

EXPECTATION MANAGEMENT

Keeping calm and remaining flexible is the name of the game. Once again, you should view such a moment as normal. The less you rely on each step of your briefing 'going according to plan,' the less stress you will have when you experience negativity, distractions, misunderstandings, and friction.

It is always good to remember that your audience, while having a right to demand an excellent product, also understands your situation and knows that walking into any organization cold can lead to awkward moments. Such moments are better seen as zero percent personal and at least 80% opportunity. It is unlikely that the sour look is because you are a failure, disliked, or don't know how to make a good presentation. It could be as simple as a command preference for black and white, double-sided copies only...or the opposite.

The opportunity lies within a little friendly confidence that might look like: "Oh (with a conversational smile), do I need to fix that product? I think it's due for an update..."

No matter what the response, at least you will know as opposed to carrying the anxiety of wondering. Plus, you will learn something about the audience and perhaps how to proceed from that point forward. Close the loop by acknowledging the concern or question as something that is going to help you be better in future presentations, i.e., constructive criticism. Even if that doesn't seem to be the spirit in which it is given.

Those are examples of the downside of new environments. The advantages are just in direct contrast to the home field as described in the previous section. There are no pre-existing issues or baggage with anyone in the room, and human nature lends itself to extending courtesy to a stranger or a guest. It is a clean slate but also an opportunity to represent your organization and increase your influence and reputation in the community.

So long as you respond to all interactions from the high ground with respect and humility you can quickly win the energy in a room of strangers to your side.

Audience 3: The Uniform Crowd

Regardless if you are playing home or away, there are plenty of other variables to consider. In both of the previous scenarios, there was one thing in common. The assumption was that the audience was comprised of Soldiers or those who work in close collaboration with Soldiers. Perhaps you could make the dynamic 50/50 soldiers and DA Civilians, but is that really a huge variable? The culture of the military is still pervasive.

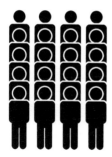 An FRG Meeting would make things a little more complicated, but what about a group of civilians from across the community who are on the installation to receive recognition from the garrison commander? In that room, you would have a range of professions, ages, and degrees of familiarity/comfort with the military. As you think about preparing some opening remarks for that event, you realize it is very different than the usual gathering on post. The next section deals with that group.

In general, the uniform or homogenous crowd is less challenging. As a Soldier, you could throw around a few acronyms and regulatory references without losing a single member of the audience. In fact, you could probably talk shop all day and get away with it. You could even tell inside jokes with people you don't even know. The uniform crowd makes life easy if you know the ropes.

On the other hand, this group will unilaterally know when you get it wrong. Not only that, but they will not extend you much grace since it behooves every service member to be "in accordance with..." and be able to cite chapter and verse. By the way, what does your uniform look like today? You can bet everyone in that audience will view you less credible because of that boot lace hanging out.

RESEARCH ALWAYS PAYS

Make sure you can deep dive into any of your main points and details from your graphics. Make sure your formats meet the current standard and check your references for dates. Even as you are reading this, there is a good chance that one of the regulations you regularly cite was just updated or amended.

You can relax with the home team, but you cannot take anything for granted.

Audience 4: The Variable Crowd

Here they are, democrats, republicans, independents, and "other" in the same room...oh, my. What can you talk about that won't cause some portion of the audience to turn on you or each other? The less homogenous your audience is, the more likely it is that any given point of your presentation will strike a wrong chord with someone. While it probably isn't your mission to make all the people happy all the time it is your mission to keep disruptions and emotions to a minimum. Once someone in the room gets their blood boiling, then your message is likely to be less effective and the time you are front and center will become a long and painful ordeal.

Look at your material. Don't just run the same slides and talking points all the time. Sure, your presentation may have been approved by your supervisor, and it may be well received in general, but that doesn't mean it is a sure bet with everyone. Use some latitude and contemplate the audience you are about to face. Look at the topics that come up and consider the implications from every walk of life.

SHARP training and Suicide training are a good example. During these training events, there are sensitive topics, examples, and discussions. Unfortunately, most participants have either experienced these issues first hand, worked with someone who experienced it, or dealt with it in their family.

The precise language that is used during these discussions can become very important. As tricky as these dialogues can be it is easy to take for granted all the advantages that standard doctrine and frequent exposure to the training convey. You can bet that if you tried to take these topics to a local high school that you would need to make quite a few changes...and not just to the army references.

BE YOURSELF
As complicated as the situation may seem, once again, it is almost instinctive to adapt your manners and words to the social situation you find yourself in. So as long as you don't auto-pilot and fail to review your material for changes, there should be few issues. It is all about the intent. What is it that you want the audience to take away and what is the simplest path there? You may be surprised how much you can cut from a questionable presentation and how much common ground you can find for all participants.

Despite surface appearances, most people share similar goals and values.

Audience 5: The Big Cheese

The setting for most briefings, especially in the military, is a small group led by a commander or ranking individual. You are there to inform everyone, but it's what the boss thinks that matters. Perhaps you just need to impress this individual with your competence on the topic. More often than not, however, there is a decision that needs to be made, information that needs to be reviewed, and a decision maker who will set a course of action in motion.

A briefing for training purposes addresses the entire audience with hopes that the boss is impressed with the material. A decision brief is more like an audience of one with several witnesses. The whole time you are a briefing, regardless of the other participants, you should remember that you are always speaking directly to the boss, and more specifically, to the boss's priorities and concerns. Other people in the room may throw out hard questions and even seem critical, but that is not because of you, it is because they are also there for one reason. They are applying their knowledge and experience for the boss's benefit. There is just no substitute for preparation and having some backup materials ready.

Of course, the cardinal rule for any commander-centric briefing is no "tap-dancing." This means that when you are caught off guard or asked about something that you have information on you do not improvise, try to assemble an answer 'on the fly', or just tell a little fib that sounds like the right answer. You may be able to fumble around a bit or bounce a question back on the audience in many settings, but not when it is this scenario.

When that uncomfortable moment occurs, you should probably take a moment and politely ask for clarification about what is being asked. This shows respect and gives your brain a moment or two to confirm that you either remember something or that you are zero balance on that quantity. The instant you realize that you are zero balance, give up all pretense of pride and accept it. Don't show the audience you are embarrassed. Just inform the commander that you do not know but that you will get the answer immediately afterward. Even if this meets some hostility, it is nothing compared to how a to tap-dance is received. Remember, no matter what happens, it happens somewhere every day and is almost never fatal. Live and learn.

Audience 6: The Panel

There are times, particularly in the higher echelons of command, in which there are a handful of individuals with an equal share of the decision-making process in the room at once. Think an X-Factor or American Idol audition. In those situations, the hopeful candidate is not auditioning for a single judge but three or four individuals who have an equal share in the outcome. You have doubtless seen these situations play out in which the entire panel may start out in opposition to the candidate, but then after some conversation and banter, a majority of board members change their minds, and then it is off to the next level.

As intense and focused as a briefing to a commander can be, it has the advantage of targeting a single individual. Something that would impress or please one commander will have the opposite effect on another. When such opposite individuals are both on the receiving end, along with one or two others, it seems you almost can't win. But, just like those first-round contestants on TV, you definitely can.

The most challenging aspect of a panel is not the diversity of the audience, but the effect of multiple counter-points. Any American attorney knows that arguing a case before the Supreme Court requires nerves and wits of steel. In that setting, you have the 12 most prominent judges in the country, hundreds of years of legal experience, and the right to interrupt your statements and responses indefinitely. You can guess what the key is. Know your stuff AND be quick to admit when you don't. The effective range of a half-baked answer is near zero and often turns on the shooter.

EXPECTATION MANAGEMENT

The real thing to remember is, what is normal? It is natural to get rattled or taken off balance by multiple authorities asking questions and digging for information. This is why promotion boards are structured in such a way. But how do you prepare for a board? Yes, you study the material, and you rehearse, but the big thing is expectation management.

Those rehearsals only tune your nerves and mentality to a new baseline of normal. The more you rehearse, the less strange the panel situation is. Being interrupted and, more or less interrogated, is not normal for most people but it also, in this context, not personal. It is just how it is. Relax, this is how it's done. Know your stuff, and give yourself a few seconds to compose your answer in your head before you start talking. It will calm your nerves, keep your information straight, and slow the momentum of the Q and A.

HECKLERS, SHARPSHOOTERS, AND ASSASSINS

This is a closely related topic to The Panel Audience from the previous section. One of the mega themes of this book is 'expectation management.' Think about the last time you were thrown off balance by an event in your personal or professional life. Think about the last time something moved you from tranquil to anger in the blink of an eye. There is a good chance that it had something to do with expectations. You can get agitated by a predictable negative, such as a smart comment from a co-worker who never has anything positive to contribute.

There is little, except discipline, that can help you overcome familiar stresses that become hot buttons of emotion. However, you can prevent your emotions and focus from derailment by Hecklers, Sharpshooters, and Assassins who are inevitably in your audience. Expecting them is half the battle. Why get rattled or take it personal when you know it's coming and you are ready for it?

EXPECTATION MANAGEMENT

There is no way to get around the fact that when you are briefing or giving a presentation, you are being evaluated; either directly, or indirectly. People will remember everything about you from your physical appearance (hair, clothes, hygiene), to your demeanor, to your organizational skills and preparation, to the way you handle interruptions and tough questions. When you keep your cool it demonstrates either supreme preparation, supreme confidence, or both. It will not be forgotten.

With that in mind, you should be disappointed if it doesn't happen... A lost opportunity to shine.

Much of what you can do to be prepared goes back to the sections that deal with personality types. If you are ready to meet the needs and the likely critiques of the major personality types, then you should feel confident.

Let's look at each type of disruptor.

Hecklers

Hecklers often do not mean much harm, but that doesn't help much when you are on the receiving end. The average heckler, in the context of work-related presentations, is usually just the office joker doing their thing. They are trying to help everyone 'lighten up' or may even think they are helping you. A good laugh or moment of nonsense is one way to relax. Maybe the heckler actually does help you, if you can laugh a little (albeit on the inside) at yourself and reply with an even comeback. However, the problem with this personality is handling them without encouraging them. If the office joker has a willing accomplice they are likely to keep rolling until the boss shuts them down. Some bosses have a high tolerance for these asides or maybe a higher tolerance than you.

EXPECTATION MANAGEMENT

The primary thing to keep in mind with the heckler, as with every other disruptor, is emotional flatness. Your presentation should have some degree of expression but seeing another person put on the spot by a critic, or heckler, brings out the natural tendency to zero in on emotional cues. It could be the sympathetic nervous system, the heightened sense that a virtual car wreck is eminent, or a more sinister motive, but you can bet your every move is radiating something about your inner state at that moment.

Emotionally flat on the outside says, 'cool and confident on the inside'.

Here are the two advantages of emotional flatness with the heckler: 1. Even if you verbally embrace the heckler and return a good, light hearted answer, you are not emotionally embracing or feeding into the heckler's actions. This goes a long way toward not encouraging the class clown. 2. The audience wants to see that you have a sense of humor, but that you are there for business. The degree to which you have a good time with a joker could translate as the degree to which you don't take the presentation seriously.

One thing to keep in mind is, what type of personality are you? Are you the office joker or the class clown? Do you heckle presenters here and there?

If so, your biggest temptation will be to go back and forth with the heckler the entire presentation. If you are not careful, you will slide into a side-bar comedy show and not even know you lost the audience. On the other hand, if you have little tolerance for clowning or joking in the workplace you will be tempted to reprimand or slam the door on the heckler. This section will address such a tactic, but using it on the heckler will usually come across as a negative.

Using the emotional flat response can be very dramatic. Perhaps your briefing style is somewhat animated or more expressive than average. If you respond to a heckler with a positive but emotionally flat statement, the contrast will definitely signal that are not interested in rabbit trails.

Sharpshooters

Now, we add the interruptions that bring some degree of malice. Don't be mistaken. You should have very high standards pertaining to your presentation, talking points, and materials. Grammatical errors, factual errors, outdated references, etc. are all a no-go and if someone calls you out, then you can be comforted in knowing that you asked for it. You should also expect that the organization you are briefing, or the audience members in particular, have high internal standards for presentations and any activity that otherwise takes away from time they need for duties and requirements.

When someone nit-picks the result of your labor and preparation, it is difficult to remain cool. There are plenty of people who can't help but poke at others a little just to see if they can take it. There are some who see the entire world as competition and want to take people down a notch when they have the opportunity. Then, on the more practical side, there are individuals whose role in the organization (a gatekeeper of some kind- think XO or Sergeant Major) requires them to be ruthless with anything or anyone that comes in front of the boss.

 EXPECTATION MANAGEMENT:
Just count on one or more of the above individuals being there: Sharpshooting is not personal, it's standard issue.

No matter how you respond, remember emotional flatness. If they mean you ill, then nothing defeats them quite like being visibly cool. If you deserve it, then taking your medicine with a no-excuses demeanor can't be beat (**and don't make excuses**, just acknowledge and move-out). If the gatekeeper puts you on blast, then accept it as mentorship and maybe even write down a quick note on the spot. People in such a position often require that others take literal notes when an issue is called out.

Assassins

Now we're getting nasty. An assassin is an individual who either doesn't like you, or is militantly against whatever it is you are selling to the audience. Maybe you are briefing the details of a controversial new policy. Anything that is perceived as creating a weaker standard will incite frustration in a good percentage of the organization. Shooting the messenger is basically an organized sport.

When an assassin interrupts or disrupts you, it is not to score points, or lighten the mood, or provoke productive conversation, etc. An assassin wants to derail you entirely and/or destroy your message. It could actually be personal, and it will always *feel* personal.

Now, more than ever, you need emotional flatness.

EXPECTATION MANAGEMENT

Again, you were expecting an assassin, right? If you are just the messenger then find a nice way to say so. If you are presenting a course of action that one person or more in the room want to squash, then be prepared to say something about how the information needs to be fully vetted. If it is for anything else, then respectfully divert it to a Q and A or discussion session at the end.

The good news is, no one likes an assassin.

Time, and the room, are on your side. Even those who agree with the assassin and their angle of attack don't like a bully. For the most part, your audience does not want to be in your shoes. They don't like to see assassins because they don't like to be on the receiving end.

> **CLASSROOM MANAGEMENT**
> Depending on your rank and the situation, you can go out on a limb and be professionally assertive with an assassin. People generally see self-defense as a right. However, make sure you have read the room correctly. For the most part, the uncomfortable, yet unspoken cloud of negative peer pressure will come to settle on the head of the disruptor.

Lowering the Boom aka. Slamming the Door

It is a technique you've seen more times than you can count. It is a technique as old as time itself. Every first-year education student learns it and you've likely employed it.

Start your presentation with a smile, wait for the first side-bar conversation or whispering voice in the audience, and then slam the door on the perpetrators.

With rare exception, there will always at least one such perpetrator. You can count on it. If your presentation is such that you can demand attentiveness (such as training) then by all means, slam the door. It works well and you can count on a courteous audience afterward.

In many cases, you are a guest, one of the lower ranking persons in the room, or trying to sell your audience on something they may not be very excited about. In such situations, door-slam technique will do little for your cause. What is more, the side-bar conversations are often between the boss and their "right-hand" or someone near the top.

In such cases, simply slow down, put a little more space between words, or humbly stop talking. This is the most natural way to "ask" the boss if they need a moment or if they have a question that you can answer. If you pause and there is no change, the silence can go from awkward to strangely disrespectful. You must know your audience, but emotional flatness come in handy again.

It might be best to just continue despite the behavior, chances are, you're getting paid either way. In most cases, the parties in question get back in the zone and offer an apology. If they ask you to repeat something they missed because they were ignoring you, then so be it. Remember, when this happens the rest of the audience will emotionally lean in your direction.

Don't Make an Example of Anyone

You probably would never plan to single out a member of your audience for scrutiny or some sort of one on one conflict during your presentation. Few things are more toxic than this sort of situation and your presentation could end abruptly. If you can resist the temptation to get your emotions involved with assassins and sharpshooters then you are gold. However, there are more innocent motives for making examples out of your audience.

Your introduction might include something that gets the audience involved, or intrigues them with a shocking fact or statistic. You need some sort of introductory moment or what educators typically call the "anticipatory set." That concept will be covered during the How portion of this book. Maybe you've seen an anticipatory set that looked something like this:

"Okay, before I get rolling into some statistics I want to really make these numbers real to you. Raise your hand if you were born between January and July"

About half of the audience raises their hands.

"Good, now just January and February."

Only a portion of the hands remain raised.

"Look around you. You are looking at roughly the number of people in an audience this size that will likely die in a car accident due to the negligence of a drunk driver."

Such an opening will probably have the desired effect of humanizing the statistics but it is impossible to not feel slightly strange if it is your hand that is raised at that moment. It is natural to feel like someone 'put that evil on your head,' or even worse, evoke the memory of a loved one who was killed by a drunk driver.

This segment of the book has been dedicated to engaging your audience on a personal level by understanding the major personality types and the sorts of concepts that keep them engaged. The big take away is 'show them you care.' If you turn anyone into an example through audience participation, then you risk sinking your connection and perhaps your message.

ART OF PERSUASION

If you plan something interactive or provocative, then design it in such a way that no one feels worse for having shown up. One way is coordinating an accomplice ahead of time. You may need a dramatic example to introduce a tragic topic, but a willing and informed actor is the way to go. If an accomplice is not possible, then engage the audience with something that puts your human examples in the winner's circle. Note a different way to conclude the anticipatory set from earlier;

"...Good, now just January and February...Congratulations! Statistically, that is the number of people in a room this size that will attempt to intervene if they see an intoxicated person attempting to drive."

See the difference? Now, that group just became virtual heroes and not at the expense of the others. Chances are, other members of the audience will go with it and high-five or laughingly compliment one of the individuals with their hands up. You can then follow up with a good question like such as;

"All games aside, has anyone here been there when someone stopped someone else from driving drunk?"

This will allow actual tales of daily heroics to enter the presentation. You can't help but evoke emotions when presenting difficult topics, but focusing on the power of people to prevent tragedy and demonstrating that it works is a positive approach.

PROJECTING YOUR ANXIETY

Most people do not enjoy giving presentations, public speaking, or generally being the center of attention. Even seasoned actors and musicians struggle with stage fright. Everyone from Adele and Demi Lovato, to the members of Green Day, Reba McEntire and a host of others admit that they have to deal with anxiety before public appearances. There is a tendency to believe that the most talented and attractive amongst us have an easy time standing center stage. This belief is rarely validated. Few things are more universal than 'nervous butterflies' prior to a presentation.

"There are only two types of speakers in the world.
1. The nervous and 2. Liars."—Mark Twain

The trouble with nervous energy is that it is often rooted in some sense that the audience may be overly critical, or that perhaps some personal shortcoming will become evident for the world to see. Something as simple as a small stain on your clothing that 'Murphy' put there just before your presentation is all it takes. If you are not careful, you can find yourself obsessed with thinking the audience is glaring at the stain when, in fact, no one sees it at all.

If this happens you will find yourself switching into a defensive or insecure posture. You will start to interpret every facial expression, every sigh, and the tone of every question in a skewed manner. You

47

could easily sense judgement where there is none or start a downward slide into the abyss of letting one mistake rattle you into another and another and another.

There will be more about this in the section that deals with stage fright, but this section deals with your audience and staying connected. This means you need to stop and think about them as just ordinary people; people like yourself. When you attend a meeting, or any aspect of your job, are you overly focused on the speaker's mistakes or the tiny shortcomings of those around you?

Yes, it can happen, but most people are too busy with their own problems to worry about you.

At any given time, each and every member of the audience is thinking about a deadline they have to meet before the end of the day, or a fight they had with their spouse, or an issue with a child, or a stiff back, a day dream, or any number of things besides you, or the stain on your shirt, or the bullet point you forgot to cover two slides ago.

Remembering that the audience just a group of people who, like you, are doing their best to get through the day in one piece is a good way to stay calm and connected.

Don't become your own heckler, assassin, or sharpshooter.

PART TWO: "WHAT"

"If you can't write your message in a sentence,
you can't say it in an hour."
—Dianna Booher

"WHAT" FAQ'S

1. My presentation covers a wide range of topics and contains a lot of information. How do organize it so that it feels focused?

    a. First, determine the one big take-away that would want the audience to retain. Next list three to five main points that are most important which support the big take-away. Third, write a concise statement that could serve as a concluding sentence for your presentation.

    b. As you look through your slides, keep those big take-away items and concluding sentence near-by. How can you alter each one to better reflect you goals? Then, shoot for the less is more approach.
        See "What is the Bottom Line" (page 51)

2. I am creating a presentation which requires me to convince my organization to invest upgrading our computers, but the leader-

ship is very cynical about it at this time. How do I put together a persuasive presentation?

    a.   You may simply go after all the positives and then address the negatives with your best salesperson instincts, but this can seem canned, dry, and predictable. You want to frame everything from their perspective and meet their intentions instead of simply presenting a good course of action.

    b.   You can use the Mark Antony model of first identifying with your audiences objections and then slowing turning those objections into support for you cause.
See "What type of presentation is it" (page 55)

3.   I normally present my material in a lecture format. What are the advantages and disadvantages of changing to question and answer or discussion format?

    a.   You can expect to cover less material, but you the topics that are covered by Q and A/discussion will resonate longer with the audience. It can also be hard to manage to flow of the discussion and maintain basic order once the audience has a hold of the reigns.

    b.   Reduce your presentation content to about three to five important points. After that, use the Socratic Approach to guide conversations in a more precise manner.
See "Questions and Discussion vs. Lecture" (page 60)

4.   My presentation is very technical and information heavy. How can I avoid overwhelming the audience as well as keep their attention?

    a.   Taking more frequent breaks is one answer but may not be feasible. Consider inserting several checks on learning. This opens up some breathing room between topics and allows you to keep your finger of the pulse of the audience.

b. You probably also want to make sure start on the right foot. Create some Q and A that you can present at the beginning to help you assess that the audience already has the pre-requisite knowledge that you think they do... Or that they are not, in fact, ready for more than you think.

See "Technical or General" (page 67)

WHAT IS THE BOTTOM LINE?

Your audience is comprised of diverse individuals with diverse person-alities, experiences, educations levels, and moods, but your message is what it is. Who you are speaking to is fundamental to the words you choose, the illustrations you use, the amount of time you spend on a single idea etc. But what are you trying to say? The bottom line is ultimately what matters. You do need to speak their language, but what is the point if you don't have crystal clear bottom line to convey?

The opening quote is about finding that single, concise idea from which your entire presentation will grow. Another famous example of this sentiment is normally attributed to Einstein; 'If you can't explain it to a six-year-old, you don't understand it yourself.' A notable caution from an individual that conveyed his ideas with advanced mathemat-ics. Even a person who struggles with long division can understand Einstein's concepts. If an advanced degree in math is necessary, then perhaps, like a dubious accountant, you are using numbers to obscure a poor idea.

Your presentation will be a small tree of knowledge. You will construct its branches and leaves according to your audiences needs and illuminate it with your presentation skills. But if it does not grow from a solid seed of a concise bottom line, then you may watch it fall over in front of you at the worst possible moment.

Stop and construct a simple, active voice sentence that states your bottom line.

Learn from Others' Mistakes

A debate concerning the value of reality-based television program-ming will likely never be resolved, but in many cases, it provides an opportunity to learn from others. Even with the cynical approach that most of what you see in a reality program is either scripted or rigged, you can still glean some practical lessons.

For the presenter, salesperson, or public speaker, there are a small slew of reality shows that focus on 'the pitch.' The dramatic pretense that keeps viewers glued to the screen is the suspense of seeing an entrepreneur sell their idea to an individual or individuals that have the resources to make their dreams a reality. Examples are Shark Tank, Billion Dollar Buyer, The Profit, West Texas Investors Club, Restaurant Start-up, and several others. People tend to be natural dreamers and wonder if they could develop an idea that would make the cut. Many people who watched American Idol secretly dreamed of wowing a crowd with their voice and, in the process, changing their life.

If you watch one of these entrepreneur-centric shows closely you may notice some trends, themes, and tendencies of the successful versus the unsuccessful. Most candidates vying for the resources of the host millionaires or billionaires have a dream, a product, a business plan, a record of sales, production methods, and a sales pitch. You may think that the sales pitch is the bottom line, but that is where the less suc-cessful candidates get hung up. In fact, this is where most people with a novel, a screenplay, a song, etc. fall off the path of success. Perhaps you've seen this play out.

What is the audiences' bottom line?

The entrepreneur takes center stage and provides the investors with samples of a product that they clearly like. The presentation style is sharp, clear, and the product looks as good as it promises to be. You are convinced that this person will have the investors fighting over the product. Then, you find out that the bottom lines do not match.

The entrepreneur thought that their brilliant product was worthy of a $500,000 investment, because it is such a great idea. Or perhaps because the product itself is so high quality, or maybe the wonderful sales pitch is enough to compel an investment. Invariably, the investors do not care about any of that. They look at the cost of production vs. the sale price and compare that ratio to the number of sales in the last several months or past year. If the numbers don't pan out or justify a $500,000 investment, then everything else is just fluff.

So, the entrepreneur's bottom line was, "I've created a great product that fills a need in the American household. It's worth a fortune."

The investor's bottom line was, "You only clear a $5.00 profit on each unit and you only sold 1000 units last year. You have grossly over-evaluated your company's worth, so no deal."

ART OF PERSUASION
As a counterpoint, even though the cameras would not like the lack of prolonged drama, the best sales pitch would match the investors bottom line from square one.

"In this small box is a product that sells for $10, costs me $1 to make, and sold 100,000 units last year. I have orders for 300,000 and my production facility is capable of doing ten times that."

At that point, the box could contain a toy rat and the investors wouldn't care. A bidding war would likely ensue.

It is an extreme example, but can you see why the first presentation failed and the second one would work. The more naïve or starry-eyed candidate will believe that an investor is looking for next big thing and therefore go all-in when they see it.

They might believe that if they can sell themselves as a worthy investment then all will be well. However, the "visionary idea" and the great salesperson are not what the investors are looking for. They are looking for a raw numerical connection between their money, the idea on the table, and potential profits.

If you have been asked to give a presentation, then there must be points of contact between your topic and the organization or audience that asked you to speak. When you mesh your bottom line with audience's bottom line your message will resonate, be remembered, and initiate change.

You may be able to easily define your own bottom line, but don't get lost in the fog of secondary factors pertaining to your audience. You need to know their *what*.

What is the single thing that defines success for this group?

What is the biggest event on this organization's short-range calendar?

What was the last thing or the thing that put this organization at the top of the heap?

Tailor your bottom line into that mold and you will, at the very least, earn respect.

WHAT TYPE OF PRESENTATION IS IT? (INFORMATIVE VS. PERSUASIVE)

Your presentation or briefing likely fits roughly into one of two categories: Informative or Persuasive. Yes, you will persuade with information and information is persuasive, but the difference is tone and therefore organization. The persuasive presentation is more interesting and challenging so it is a good place to start.

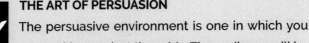

THE ART OF PERSUASION
The persuasive environment is one in which you are working against the odds. The audience will be somewhere between cynically disinterested in your topic and violently in opposition. Your goal is to change their minds and bring them to your side. A sales presentation will often fall into this category. Persuasion may be an art and some may see it as pure manipulation, but there is at least one formula that can give you a fighting chance even if it seems manipulative on the surface.

The Persuasive Presentation

Friends, Romans, countrymen, lend me your ears...

Sound familiar? Those are the opening words of what is arguably the best persuasive speech of all time. It is in the third act of Shakespeare's Julius Caesar and the speaker is Mark Antony. The context of the speech is important, because it falls into the far end of the spectrum in which the audience is **violently** opposed to the message.

Caesar had just been murdered on the senate floor and the Roman mob seemed very pleased with that result. To make matters worse, Antony was not particularly liked or trusted amongst the populace. Despite this, Mark Antony attempted to not only give Caesar a glowing eulogy, but also convince the mob to change their tune from 'death to Caesar' to 'down with Caesar's murderers.' Feint hearts need not apply for this briefing assignment.

If Mark Antony can succeed in this setting, then most other settings seem less challenging by comparison. He was successful and here is the basic format he used.

- **Antony stated his innocent intentions**

   "I come to bury Caesar, not to praise him."

   Or, don't worry, I'm not going to say nice things about this guy you all hate. I'm just going to take care of the task at hand.

- **Antony agreed with the crowd's opinions**

   "The noble Brutus hath told you Caesar was ambitious:

   If it were so, it was a grievous fault..."

   The crowd believed, thanks in large part to an earlier speech by "noble Brutus," that Caesar's ambitions made him a threat to the Roman Republic. Antony saw that Brutus was well received so he chose to compliment Brutus and agreed that ambition was likely Caesar's great sin.

- **Antony casts doubt on the negative message**

   "When that the poor have cried, Caesar hath wept:

   Ambition should be made of sterner stuff: Yet Brutus says he was ambitious; And Brutus is an honorable man."

   The idea isn't too complicated. Antony mentions one of Caesar's virtues, then contrasts it with ambition and shrugs his shoulders. 'well, Brutus says Caesar was ambitious and Brutus in an honorable man, so it must be so.' As the speech proceeds through several such passages you can almost feel the crowd doubting both Caesar's ambition and Brutus' honor.

- **Antony invokes the crowd's previous feelings and beliefs**

"You all did love him once, not without cause:

What cause withholds you then, to mourn for him?"

Note the timing of this message. It could be tempting to lead with this one. If, in fact the people once loved Caesar, then why not say to the angry mob, "Hey everyone, calm down. You loved him once, remember?" It is probably hard to see that resonating with the crowd at that time. Instead, he worked them into a place where they would reflect on the past in his context.

- **Antony expresses his true feelings openly and the crowd agrees with him.**

"And men have lost their reason. Bear with me;

My heart is in the coffin there with Caesar,

And I must pause till it come back to me."

The transition is from, 'Don't mind me, I'm not here to mourn, just fulfill my duties. You guys are right about Caesar,' to, 'This death is a tragedy that we must mourn together.' Of course, Antony intended to turn the crowd in his favor from the very beginning, but he gets credit for doing it so well against such great odds.

The art of persuasion is fundamental to several professions and useful to everyone at some point in their life. The Mark Antony model is held in high regard, but it is not an end all solution. A template of some kind is preferable when faced with the unenviable task of convincing one person, or a group of people, to adopt an idea or point of view they oppose.

Beyond your template, effective communication is the real goal. As such, persuasion will require you to keep the fundamentals in mind.

- Research your audience
- Actively listen to participants
- Courtesy and respect always
- Keep Cool
- Anticipate objections and critiques
- Know your subject in depth

EXPECTATION MANAGEMENT
You may want total victory, but don't make it non-negotiable. The inevitable result of that mind-set is an overly aggressive approach and escalating emotions. Simply opening a door two while preserving your position as a rational and approachable subject matter expert provides a route to the long-term win.

THE INFORMATIVE PRESENTATION

The informative presentation is far more common since organizations thrive on gathering, consolidating, discussing, and deciding on information. Training is another form of providing an information brief. The setting is straight forward with an audience that arrives ready to receive data that either they themselves requested or will be held accountable to later. In other words, an adversarial process isn't necessary.

Whereas a persuasive brief has an undercurrent of intrigue and human drama, the information brief almost guarantees something dry or dull. Therein lies your challenge.

Your audience knows why they are there and have probably heard much of what you will say on a prior occasion. A few participants will have some genuine interest in your topic, but many are there out of obligation and did not want to leave what they were doing to come hear the presentation.

Just because it may be challenging to make the briefing interesting doesn't mean you need to find some innovative or dynamic way to pull it off. Your organization, or the nature of the brief, may require that you keep things low key and direct. The How section of this book will cover the ins and outs of making things more interesting and the following segment on Q and A is a good place to start, but one fundamental always helps; brevity.

Are you 'training to time' or 'training to standard.' If you MUST fill a certain block of time, then try to avoid doing so with what is often called 'fluff.' Fluff is information that is either marginally important or simply a review of things your audience already knows. If you want to reserve some space at the end as a place for audience questions, then be prepared for the possibility that there will be only one or none. If the setting facilitates an early dismissal, then that is great. If not, then you just set yourself up for a period of awkward silence, or some form of impromptu tap dancing. In other words, allocate time with caution.

If you are training to standard, then you can streamline for maximum effectiveness. Do not cut content down to the point where your audience knows that you wanted to get this over with even more than they did and therefore went for the absolute minimum. Somehow, ten minutes of this briefing feels like more of a waste of time than an hour of genuine (even if redundant) instruction.

An optimal approach is to ruthlessly cut everything that is both old news AND not mandated. Then, find those three to five topics or points that are most important or new and go into as much depth as possible.

You should provide a review of the older information and leave some room to cover portions in depth if the need arises.

Demonstrating that you know what's unimportant, while simultaneously putting some depth and passion into the main points, will convey professionalism and respect for the audiences' time.

Questions and Discussion vs. Lecture

What do you like better, a two-way discussion format, or a lecture? A bit of both? A safe answer might be, 'it depends.' There are topics that lend themselves to each approach. Your own answer would vary depending on the speaker, the topic, or even your mood. So now, it's up to you. What are you going to do?

You could be in a situation where much of your content and format is directed. If so, then this section will discuss the ups and downs of each approach for your consideration. Otherwise, consider your audience, the time available, and your goals for the presentation.

Q and A / Discussion Format

The question and answer format is the preferable format in almost any context. It facilitates discussion, which facilitates the audiences' investment in the content, which in turn increases attention span and retention of the briefing content. However, this format limits the amount of information you can cram into your allotted time, requires confidence and skill in front of an audience, and is more difficult to manage and keep on track.

RESEARCH ALWAYS PAYS

To utilize the question and answer method correctly it might help to have your head in the right place as you plan your questions and possible responses to the answers. The guiding philosophy for the discussion format is the Socratic Method. Law schools take particular pride in adhering to the Socratic Method in their instruction, but most teachers employ it to some degree. The method is designed to foster critical thinking and masters of it can walk a debate opponent into trap after trap. It is only effective if you know your topic and have invested your own critical thought into it.

The Socratic Method also fosters discovery as opposed to simply hearing. You likely remember your own "eureka moments" far longer than most things handed to you in a lecture. If you can guide your audience into discovering facts or truths for themselves they will feel invigorated by the topic your present.

Examples of the Socratic Method in action are easy to find. Most court room dramas revolve around witness testimony and cross examination. Usually, the attorney sets the witness up with some easy questions that do not seem threatening and then the answers to first questions slowly come back to haunt the witness as the attorney closes the trap.

You approach will be different because you are not out to be your audience's adversary or accuser. Think more in terms of finding ways to make your audience tell you what you wanted to tell them. Look at this example of lecture method.

Lecture or Narrative Method: "Drinking responsibly is important. Your career could easily be at stake if you make a bad decision with alcohol. It might surprise you to know that law enforcement gives out around one million citations for driving while intoxicated in the United States every year. But there are worse things. One in three fatalities on the road are alcohol related and, on average, this equals about one death every 45 minutes."

That's not bad. Those are, well, sobering statistics. People have different degrees of experience with alcohol and the unintended consequences. For many people the 'mistakes' they made while drinking amount to a handful of humorous stories and fond memories. Meanwhile, others know all too well how deadly and destructive alcohol can be. No matter where people are on the spectrum they will likely nod with some sense of interest and then move on.

The Socratic Method might have a greater impact.

Instructor: "Who knows the odds of winning the lottery?"
Audience: "One in a billion...One in ten million...One in 100 million....etc"

Instructor: "Well, it does depend on which lottery, but the big one in our state is one in 300 million. Okay, now, how many people do you think get arrested every year for driving while intoxicated?"

(Two seemingly unrelated questions get the audience thinking about where the connection is. They are already engaged, paying attention, and thinking critically.)

Audience: "100 million...200,000...etc"
Instructor: "About one million. And about how many people are killed in alcohol related accidents every year?"

(They are still trying to make the connection to the lottery)

Audience: "5000...1000...50000...etc."
Instructor: "Almost 10,500. Now, 1 Million tickets for drunk driving and 10,500 deaths related to drunk driving. If there are 320 million people in this country, then what are the odds for anyone of us falling into

that category? I'll let someone who's brave enough to work out a little math take a crack at it." Always have these answers ready. Don't count on your audience to do math and don't wait too long for answers.

Audience Member: "Okay, so, one in 325 for a ticket and one in... 31,000 for dying, right?"
Instructor: "That's close enough. But...What are your odds if you simply refuse to drive after drinking?"

That last question might feel like the "gotcha" moment because it turns the questions around. But we're not there yet.

Audience Member: "So what are you trying to say, we're like, a hundred million times more likely to get arrested for drunk driving than get rich in the lottery?"
Instructor: "Nope. My point is you have a one in 300 million chance of winning the lottery, but how many lottery winners ever bought anywhere close to 300 million tickets? Odds can create false views of risks and rewards." (That's lowering the Socratic boom) "As we go over some facts and statistics I want you to remember Lisa Quam. She's not a victim of drunk driving, she was a resident of Washington State and won the big jackpot with the only ticket she ever bought. Not only that, but she was Washington State's first winner. Whenever you make a bad decision or take a chance, don't think about the odds, think about Lisa Quam. It only takes once."

One thing should stand out as the biggest difference between the Socratic approach and the lecture approach; time. As dry as the lecture paragraph was, it was also brief. Leading individuals down the Socratic path requires both finesse and a few dedicated moments to get the ball rolling. Of course, there is a different pay off and an entirely different engagement with your audience.

You need to do a cost to benefit analysis according to time available and material that must, at a minimum, be covered. An entire presentation conducted in a Socratic method is rare for reasons already discussed, but it is a great way to embellish your briefing and keep the audience engaged. Whether you have more time than material or simply recognize that two or three points of your presentation warrant audience participation, you should consider the Socratic approach.

How Not to Do Q and A

The question and answer approach does not have to be elaborate or artful. There is nothing wrong with throwing in a few ordinary response opportunities to make sure the audience stays awake and break the monotony. You are far better off doing this than leaving the question-and answer-aspect entirely out of your briefing.

To prevent yourself from conducting question and answer ineffectively, just reflect on presentations, classes, or training that made you want to walk out every time the presenter asked a question. Bad Q and A is painful because it is lifeless.

Lifeless questions fall into two categories; pointless and obvious.

Pointless:

"So, this is when the 101st Airborne Division was getting ready to advance into Iraq. Has anyone ever served in the 101st?...one? two? A few? Ok. (Awkward pause)...The Brigade commanders were briefed that..."

A pointless question either promises to lead somewhere and does not (above). Of simply inspires no one to respond.

"This was formerly under USAG. Anyone heard of USAG? Ok. But now falls under IMCOM. Anyone want to work for IMCOM? Ok. As you can see..."

Obvious:

"And so SHARP violations are bad for the force, right? Yes? No? SHARP issues hurt our ability to accomplish the mission, yes? No?"

There certainly is a context in which an audience deserves obvious questions, but obvious questions usually just garner irritated nods and blank expressions. Your goal for introducing Q and A is to stimulate conversation, participation, and critical thinking.

Don't worry about being a master of the Socratic Method, but if you are adding question just to add questions, it will simply do more harm than good.

LECTURE FORMAT—SEEK CLARITY

The audience is captive, the floor is yours, and you have the thankless task of keeping your presentation interesting and applicable. The briefing that consists almost entirely of a lecture format is direct, inherently authoritative, and time conscious. You can shine by using this time efficiently as opposed to abusing it.

If you keep one word in mind while preparing your presentation and your notes, it should be clarity. Military culture demands concise, active language which is great training for effective lecture settings. Active voice set within well-organized short sentences will always shine.

How would you change this passage if it were your job to present it to an audience?

"This is one of the things we need to cover today. The proper wear of branch insignia on the new uniform is different from what you are used to or might have been expecting. Note these measurements and compare them to old measurements on the current dress uniform. There is a full quarter inch difference between the two. This is something you might take for granted if you aren't careful because, so many other measurements are the same as the current uniform."

Okay, that was overly terrible. But a nervous or unprepared instructor might not sound so different from that very passage. Here is one possible revision:

First topic: "Proper wear of the branch insignia. Note, 1/8-inch measurement above the seam. A subtle but important change. If your Soldiers are in a hurry or just don't care, then this is one place it will show."

This revision makes the right assumptions in terms of showing the audience respect. Whereas the first iteration wastes time on obvious or trivial points, the revision assumes that the audience can read (the slide deck), that they know the current standard, and that they care mostly about their role as a leader.

ART OF PERSUASION

When you speak, you produce subtle clues that reveal how you see yourself, the world, and your audiences' overall character. A room full of NCOs receiving a mandatory overview of proposed uniform changes would quickly tune out, or loose respect for, the instructor based on the first version. They would not be able to outline why the speaker's language was putting them at edge, but the silent sentiment in the room would vary between, 'does this guy think we're stupid?' to 'this clown is wasting our time.'

Additionally, you can count on the audience's thoughts wandering in direct proportion to how often you wander around a main point.

The lecture format does not have to be boring or ineffective. Decide the main or three main points you want your briefing to communicate. Then, look at each slide or chart and identify the single thing the audience should learn from it. After that, write down a few words or sentences that describe how the audience should see themselves in your presentation. From that skeleton, you should be able to build an effective, compelling lecture.

TECHNICAL OR GENERAL

If you are a presenter, then you are by default a teacher. Your job is to either introduce new information or reinforce previously discussed or understood material. There are many challenges to teaching in any context, but one of the paramount problems is understanding the space between your own understanding of the content and the audiences understanding.

For example, a new teacher who stands before a room full of 1st graders for the first time is prepared to teach some basics about addition. The teacher has utilized basic addition for decades and completed many years of mathematical training and applications. As they begin the instruction can they really remember, or even imagine, just how alien the basics of math can be to a young mind?

Most new teachers experience many "ah-ha" moments during their first year as they learn, to their own despair, that they have been talking above their students' heads more often than not.

While it is unlikely that the gulf of knowledge between you and your audience equals that between a college graduate and a 1st grader, it is still a reality that you must appreciate. You will want to rush into the "good stuff" and gloss over your own lead-up talking points. Then, there is the natural tendency to think that others generally know what you know and encounter the same streams of information that you do.

Questions can help you quickly assess the gap.

Near the start of any presentation, you should build in a few questions that give you a quick read on how much your audience actually knows. You may discover that they know far less or far more than you expect. By the same token, you may never find an audience that matches your expectation of base-line knowledge.

Think about that.

 EXPECTATION MANAGEMENT
A few questions such as the following can dramatically impact the effectiveness of what you are about to present. What is more, they will help you avoid alienating your audience by starting on the wrong foot.

- "Who can tell me about this graphic?"
- "How would you finish this sentence?"
- "If you were given this problem, what is the first thing you would do?"
- "Raise your hand if you've heard of..."
- etc.

The bottom line is that any attempt to transfer knowledge from your head to another person will always be a challenge. Identifying the gaps between you and your audience is the best way to start.

Here are some other things to consider when toggling between technical details or general information.

Technical

Your task may be to convey highly technical or detailed information, but is your audience ready for it? Are they as ready for it in the format and depth that you have prepared?

You've likely heard the phrase "drinking from the firehose," and there are plenty of times when it is both necessary and unavoidable. However, have you ever crammed for an exam after ignoring the course content for the previous week, month, or semester? Regardless of how well you did on the test, how much of that content did you know a week later?

Even if your audience is smart and informed you will lose them one by one if you push technical details too hard or too fast. People "space out" for moments here and there. Their minds wander. They daydream. They contemplate rabbit trail ideas based on what they see in front of them. Hence, they will all miss one or more talking points.

However, one of the last things people do, is admit they are lost or that you are going too fast or talking above their heads. No doubt, there are individuals who speak up, but by the time they do you may have lost the entire room.

The answer is to perform frequent checks on learning.

Every segment of a presentation should include an opportunity to engage the audience, but the more technical your content, the more frequently this should be done. There are two benefits to checks on learning. 1) It provides a pause and 2) it provides a moment of mandatory audience involvement. There are always a handful of people who are too shy to stop a presentation to admit they are confused, but a quick Q and A session allows people to tag onto an answer or interject questions and comments.

For Example, you might ask a yes or no question about the first chart, but then as the question gets answered a hand will pop up and bring up another topic. Checks on learning provide a break in the formality and open up a door to your audience's understanding. But don't just plan checks on learning, plan to adjust or revisit entire segments as a result.

Be Flexible.

CLASSROOM MANAGEMENT
No matter who you are, technical information is exhausting. You and your team could spend your lives pouring over numbers and talking non-stop techno-babble. That doesn't mean that a group event in which a third party (you) are setting the context and the pace is easy to absorb. Aren't you there to challenge them and introduce something new?

Be deliberate and watch your pace. Constantly scan the audience for confused or vacant looks. Everyone learns at different rates and learning styles will vary.

The final word about technical information is actually the preliminary word; rehearse. Run your presentation by someone who represents your audience. They can provide you with the feedback that lets you know if you are on target. There is almost always a difference between what you think you are saying and what you are actually saying.

General

Oh good, just a general view of the topic. This will be easy. The trouble is, generalities are generally a bad thing. Speaking in generalities is often associated with spin, lack of knowledge, manipulation, tap-dancing, propaganda, etc. So never do it, right?

Not quite.

Generalities are actually an important aspect of communication. Without them, all instruction would devolve into an endless graduate dissertation. Generalities are suitable when discussing terms, concepts, or content that is already accepted, understood, and agreed upon.

Your task might be to provide an overview or review of previous events or content. Perhaps you are trying to prompt discussion or challenge assumptions. There are always suitable times to use generalities. Generalizing is also acceptable if you are sharing your own experiences and observations relative to the subject i.e. "Generally speaking, most NCOs I've worked with…"

:) **BE YOURSELF**
If you are honest with yourself, you will be honest with your audience. Trying to gloss over a shortfall in research or preparation with a well phrased generality is a deliberate act. You may be eloquent enough to pull it off, but it will be noticed.

Regardless of the intent of your presentation, always be prepared to back up every generality with details. If there is anything on your charts that you don't understand then you are waiting for an awkward moment.

"Hidden slides," supplemental materials, and rehearsals are all good ideas.

There is always one person out there who likes to probe into even the most proven and accepted generality just to make sure you know your stuff. If you answer confidently and correctly, then you can count on some slack later on when you need it.

WHAT YOU WANT TO INCLUDE BUT SHOULD LEAVE OUT

You've probably seen one or two "director's cut" movies. These revised versions of the film usually add a few or several scenes that were cut from the original film. There are instances in which the director's cut actually doubles the run-time of the movie. True fans of the film enjoy seeing these additions and even discover that some of their favorite scenes can only be found in the director's cut. However, in time, most viewers gravitate back toward the original film. It is a tug of war between ideas and scenes that the director was emotionally attached to vs. the most streamlined and concise telling of a story.

Do not give your audience the director's cut.

That hilarious video clip you found last week and your favorite meme are begging to be shared with more of the world, and you are certain you can find a way to fit them into your presentation. Certainly, there is always room for a quote from your favorite celebrity, philosopher, or politician. It won't come across as controversial, will it? Anytime can be a good time to reference words of wisdom from your religious tome of choice, right? It won't be pushy, it will be profound...Certainly. And don't forget those amazing extra facts you discovered while doing your research that would demonstrate how thoroughly you looked into this and know your stuff. That would fit right in with dropping the name of a high ranking general or public personality you once worked with. Everyone likes that, don't they?

Each and every member of your audience has their own unique blend of cultural exposure, religious beliefs, and ideas about humor. Inserting your own personal mix into otherwise informative or persuasive presentation will detract from both the content and the audience's connection with you.

The other temptation you will often face when it comes to extra "director's cut" material falls into the category of making sure your story is told. Yes, you do want the audience to understand your content, but facts speak for themselves. It is more of an art, but your gut instinct should tell you when you are overselling something.

If you've ever seen a salesman turn you off of a product or a purchase decision by pushing the talking points too hard or too long, you know you don't want to be that person.

If you have passion or believe in the topic it will show, people will notice and they will respond. As a bonus, you will doubtless be ready for anything during any Q and A.

ACCORDING TO WHO?—HAVE YOUR SOURCES HANDY

The first source you find on the internet is always the most accurate.
—Abraham Lincoln

Is there something wrong that quote?

Is there anything right about that quote?

As blatantly ridiculous as that is, imagine posting something that looks equally ridiculous to a subject matter expert but looks completely legitimate to you. In the context of briefing army leaders, you might know how tenuous it can be to quote regulations. It is easy to accidentally quote an outdated regulation or miss the latest updates, but there is always someone out there who will spot it.

Things will get particularly dicey when posting anything out of date regarding sexual harassment, suicide, gender, etc. If you are going to quote a guiding authority for your organization be sure you have read the quote or segment in context and from the latest publication.

Maybe your topic is something less controversial like basic nutrition. Maybe you've heard of the food pyramid. What does the latest version look like? Probably not like you remember it. What about the other nutritional guidelines like Myplate.

What does the Army recommend as a guide? Is that different from the other branches of service? The point is that you might be showing the latest recommendations from the USDA but if the Army has hard and fast criteria that are different from what you are showing, you will look like the Abraham Lincoln quote above.

RESEARCH ALWAYS PAYS

The final thing to check is that you have your sources, in full, available during your presentation. You might have a physical copy behind your notes, you might have it on digital copy, or perhaps a series of links on a slide which you can access. You don't want to be a wise guy or patronize the audience in defensive mode. However, sometimes, it may be necessary to pull up the source.

If it ever comes to that you will score heroic levels of credibility if you can a) produce the source as needed and b) confidently read the sections in question with the knowledge that you've already verified it.

Be careful with internet sources even if they are from accepted credible sites. Maybe it is a government website or a major news organization. You know that most of the time you can return to those sites a week, month, or year from now and discover that, like a book on the shelf, nothing has changed. But Murphy's law dictates that the majority of live performances will be the exception.

News organizations update, edit, redact, and even retract their online news articles. A key passage you cited last week might simply be gone today. Websites are prone to broken links, crashes, hacks, construction, redirects, reprogramming, and ever evolving policies and protocols.

There are a multitude of reasons why the webpage you are looking for will no longer be available or look completely different when you revisit it. Best advice: Print, date, and file your internet sources. It also would not hurt to revisit them from time to time if you plan on giving the same presentation several times over the course of weeks or months.

PART THREE: "WHERE"

As an artist, environment has a lot of impact on choices, and
these choices can change by changing your location.
—Ashkan Kooshanejad

"WHERE" FAQ'S

1. This will be my first presentation in an auditorium. Is there anything I should be aware of besides expecting a lot more faces in my audience?

    a. You should consider both the way you use physical space during your presentation and if you are new to using a microphone and/or multiple screens. Rehearse under live conditions so that you can get a feel for the lights, the physical location of your charts relative to you, and the best way to use the physical space available to you on the stage.

    b. Auditoriums also mean more lights, speakers, microphone, computer, mixing board, etc. to worry about. There are a lot of things that can go wrong. You need to feel confident that you check conditions shortly before your presentation and that you know who to contact if there are problems.
    See "Board Room vs. Auditorium" (Page 82)

2. I'm the super-star presenter in my organization. Why should I worry about giving a presentation as a guest at a new location?

    a. The things you take for granted may set you off balance. And if you are used to being flawless and in control, then it may not take more than a couple of unexpected issues to shake your confidence.

    b. Are you really ready to take your show on the road? What sort of set up are you used to? What if the new location has monitors to display your digital products? Do you know who to contact for any issues with the equipment or the room when you arrive? Are your digital products ready for the new locations cyber security, or do you need to provide them in advance? What else are you forgetting? See "Home vs Away" (page 80)

LOCATION, LOCATION, LOCATION

The quote from Ashkan Kooshanejad may not seem so relevant since it is in reference to being an "artist" and the source is a professional musician. But if anyone knows something about handling an audience, it is a professional musician.

Musicians, or at least the successful ones, manage to not just get people to show up and listen to them, but convince those same people to pay for the privilege of doing so. More interestingly, some portion of the audience is made up of repeat customers who don't mind paying multiple times to hear the same show repeatedly.

The most pertinent part of the quote deals with making choices and making changes based on location. Location can and probably should change some or all of a planned presentation. Everything from your choice of clothing, to display mediums, presentation style, body language, voice projection, etc. might be impacted by the location of your briefing.

Some of ideas in this section were touched on in previous segments, but the next few sections will delve into details and considerations that could prove to be game changers for better or worse and are best not taken for granted.

Go back to the example of a professional musician for a moment. Compare a nightclub setting to the stadium. What differences would you expect in terms of equipment? What are the differences in how to engage a crowd? Which performance would you expect to be more casual? What would you expect in terms of using the stage (performing in a small area vs. moving around from end to end.)?

The answers are fairly obvious but that is the point. Despite the fact that location changes everything, it is easy to think that a straightforward briefing or presentation about the latest product, policy, requirement, or innovation is less subject to the realities of venue. Maybe, but not usually.

HOME VS. AWAY

The introduction encouraged you not to take anything for granted regarding location, and your "home field" is why you might be tempted to so anyway. If you have been asked to brief at another location, then the chances are you are one of the "hometown heroes" when it comes to presentations. Or maybe you just have to slog around the big table with the boss twice a week along with all your peers. Either way, you are comfortable and confident with presenting your material, addressing the audience, working the room, and handling any surprises or issues that drop in unexpectedly.

When it comes to the home field there are more dynamics you take for granted than you likely appreciate. You know what the condition the room will be in when you arrive because you pass by it on a regular basis. You know who the points of contact are for reserving the room and getting it rearranged. You know how to switch back and forth between screens and turn on all the equipment. You know what temperature to expect, where the thermostat is, the changes of light and temperature throughout the day.

You probably even know if the briefing/conference room is always the hottest/coldest room in the building. You know how many chairs are available and where to get extras. You probably even can connect your personal files to the shared drive in the conference room's computer.

- How much of that, and more, is pertinent to your success during an important presentation?

- How much of that will you think about when preparing to brief a new location?

  Then there are the other dimensions you might not appreciate.

- When you need the conference room in your organization you probably just informally mention it to right POC in the office next to you and lock it in.

- Who does that at the new location? How much lead time do they need?

- If you need more copies on site will you be able to use their machine? Do they have one?

- How do you transfer your presentation to their computer?

- Maybe all their computers are restricted from reading CDs and you have to deliver it to the IT manager a week ahead of time.

- Does all their equipment work? Maybe the monitors are out or maybe the PA system is known for being static-ridden and breaking sound up.

- Are you used to moving around when you brief? Is there room for that at the new venue?

- Are you used to a podium? Will they have one there?

- If you inspect the room for proper setup a day ahead of time how do you know it will stay that way? Who oversees that sort of thing?

- What events are taking place at that location prior to your presentation?

- Is there another even immediately after yours? What about immediately before?

These are some of the things that you might never think too much about in your organization but never have the same answers or expectations at other locations.

When it comes to setting up any event at a new or unfamiliar location the need to start early and check often is hard to overemphasize. The earlier you start the more likely you are to gain the cooperation and good graces of the person or persons that make things happen at that facility. Which is good, because there is an old saying that goes something like, 'a failure to plan on your part does not constitute an emergency on mine.' Being on the receiving end of that sentiment is not a great way to go into an event where you are in the spotlight.

It never hurts to ask the 'go to' person in your own organization, "What am I forgetting?"

BOARD ROOM VS. AUDITORIUM

This comparison goes back to the musician example from the last section. You don't necessarily need to fill the space that you are given, but you do need to command it. Standing behind a podium and pointing at bullet points on a nearby screen is a tight, professional way to deliver a presentation in the board room, but a loser on the auditorium stage.

Most auditoriums are designed with crowd worthy presentations in mind. There are typically built in screens or at least one large screen. They have a healthy array of lights focused on the stage. There is usually at least on podium but sometimes two. Expect to find both plugs and some form of PA system for microphones.

Briefing in an auditorium setting is not the norm for most staff professionals. So let's take a look at each of those elements and their implications.

- **Screens**
  - One or two? Do you want the same thing on each or two different but coordinated images?
  - Do they both work? How do you get your product on to the computer or other device that controls them?
  - Do you normally brief with the screen in front of you or to your side? What happens when it is above your head and or behind you?
  - Will you need extra practice to adjust your briefing style to the placement of the graphics?

- **Lights**
  - Everyone likes extra sets of bright lights in their face when they are engaged in public speaking (just kidding of course). Are you ready for that? Do you plan to rehearse with all the lights on?
  - Is there a major difference in room temperature between the stage and the rest of the room?
  - Do you see yourself needing more water than usual nearby to prevent a dry throat? Maybe you normally don't think about water but now you should.
  - Will the actual presentation involve a darkened auditorium? If so, how well will you be able to see the audience's reactions and level of interest?

- **Microphones and PA Systems**
  - When was the last time you presented with a microphone?
  - Do you know the right distance to keep it from your mouth?
  - Do you have extra batteries for a clip-on microphone?
  - How about back-up microphones?
  - What causes feedback?
  - What resolves feedback?
  - If your microphone ultimately fails how loud do you really have to be to compensate?
  - Who will run the sound system and assist with any audio-visual issues?
  - Will that person be at your rehearsal?
  - Do you have any voice inflections, or habits such as over enunciating or under enunciating that will play terribly through a microphone?

More about microphones:

You are about to learn why the military and law enforcement utilize phonetic alphabets i.e. "This is Alpha 21. Read you Delta 6." The answer is the peculiar reality of microphones.

Most people do not know that microphones are strange animals. They do not have a brain so they cannot interpret sound. As bizarre as this concept sounds it is important. When people talk to you they tend to hit consonants in a rather lazy way. For instance, the "t" in "cat" is usually a soft stop of air flowing upward as opposed to a biting, crisp "t" as in "tack." The second or third consonants are usually under-enunciated. Note those same two words and think about how you pronounce the "k" sound in tack vs. the same "k" sound at the start of Cat. The place-ment of the consonant at the start invites a crisp attack. The one at the end is almost an afterthought.

Your brain is constantly compensating for soft enunciations, slurs, and wildly varying pitch and volume fluctuations in the course of a single sentence. You use your innate understanding of context, language, and communication styles to fill in the gaps.

A microphone cannot do this, and it cannot learn your accent or dialect no matter how long you talk. You might be able to understand a strong accent or regional dialect after working with someone for a short period of time but that is just your brain doing great things automatically.

A microphone has a tendency to remove those subtle cues that help people fill in the gaps and when you say "cat" with a soft stop on the "t" the microphone will likely produce a crisp and clear "can"

RESEARCH ALWAYS PAYS

Sometimes, you need to research your own habits. If you are going to use a microphone and are not used to it, then practice speaking just a little bit slower and speaking with crisp or blunt consonants. Think about how subtle the difference between "M" and "N" is (Hence the phonetic military Mike and November).

If you tend to use lively tones that toggle between low and high or soft and loud, just expect to see a few jolts and shocked facial expressions. Microphones don't smooth over dynamic changes...at all (this is one of the answers to 'what causes feedback'). That doesn't mean be monotone, but appreciate the fact that a more subdued and professional approach to tone and volume is needed. Why do you think news anchors talk the way they do?

At the same time, if you tend to be pretty steady but always talk loud, then plan to keep the microphone placement low. The opposite is true if you know you are soft spoken. Whatever you do, don't plan on trying to find the right level when you are live. Rehearsals with microphones help you know what level you need as soon as you hit the stage: One quick adjustment and then you are rolling.

EXPECT CLIMATE PROBLEMS (DRESSING FOR THE WEATHER IS A GOOD START BUT BRIEFING AREAS HAVE THEIR OWN WEATHER SYSTEMS)

"It's freezing in here."

How many times have you heard or said that at the start of a briefing inside an auditorium or large conference room? What did it feel like a half hour after all the seats were filled and the audio-visual equipment was in full gear? What did it feel like at the end?

Another way to look at it is, how many times did the room temperature begin at a perfect temperature and conclude with everyone wiping the sweat from their brow?

Welcome to the art and science of dealing with room temperature during presentations and briefings. It's time to think about managing your own climate needs, preparing for climate room, knowing how to respond to climate changes, and reading the effect of climate on the audience.

Preparation: Because Proactive Solutions are Always the Best

First question is, have you ever briefed in this venue before or been in the audience? If you have and you don't remember thinking about the room temperature, then the room temperature was good. Someone planned for success and created the appearance of seamless environmental control.

Because the point is to make sure your audience has their mind on you and your topic as opposed to the weather.

An audience full of people fanning themselves with the hands, programs, or hats, is an audience that will remember little to anything substantive from the program.

RESEARCH ALWAYS PAYS
Find out who runs the show or normally sets up the room for presentations and ask them what to expect and what can be done to mitigate routine issues. In most government settings, there is little to anything you can do to change the thermostat since a central authority decides when you can run heat or AC as well as the temperature range you will work in. Perhaps it saves money on installation energy expenses, but it doesn't have to leave you without options.

Windows, doors, time of day, the daily forecast, and number of people that will attend are important factors.

As a scientific principle, air flows in order to balance the difference between cool and warm spaces. This means that if your office is 74 F and the hallway is 70 F, then you can expect the air in your office to draft out into the hallway when you open your office door. Incidentally, this is precisely why you never want to open a door when a fire is suspected on the opposite side.

So what?

Scenario: It is May 20th and the installation has determined that the air conditioner in your building will not be active until the 1st of June. It is 78 degrees with no wind and by the end of the day it will feel like 80 in your conference room. You are scheduled to provide a one hour presentation for 25 people in the late afternoon which will fill your conference area to near capacity.

You already know that there will be a problem, so what are your options to mitigate the issue.

Possibilities:

- Move the presentation to an earlier time of day: Usually not possible but sometimes it is more than welcome and people will jump at the opportunity (Fridays, for example).

- Request permission to use authorized uniform modifications during the presentation. Simultaneously, if individuals will be in civilian attire then advise participants as soon as possible that more temperate attire is encouraged. This allows them to prepare ahead of time.

- See if you can present the material at a larger venue within your organization. A larger room mitigates the tendency for an audience to heat up the space.

- Open doors and windows well ahead of the presentation and keep them open during the presentation (if security permits). You want an optimum and even temperature at the start of the presentation with as much "fresh air" as possible. Later, when the conference room picks up one to five degrees above the temperature of the other rooms it will create a natural draft and air will flow in and out of the room.

- Remember, a lack of centralized air flow from the ventilation system will also create a concentration of carbon dioxide in enclosed spaces. While not deadly, per se, CO_2 does invite the "sleep monster."

- Fans! Fans are the most common solution and usually available. Most facilities even have a few of giant variety that resemble stage wind machines. But how to employ them. Most people want the fan blowing right on them, but collectively, you are better served if they are at the doors or windows to multiply any natural draft. If you have two entrances try the push-pull method of one fan blowing fresh air in at one door and a second fan pulling warm air out through the other door. You can't fool natural processes, but you can enhance them.

- How loud are the fans? How distracting will the additional sound be? What can you do to mitigate?

- If possible and permissible, have ice cold water, juice, or soda available. You don't necessarily want to encourage an abundance of latrine breaks but holding a cold can or bottle usually makes people feel cooler even if they don't drink the contents.

WHAT TO EXPECT WHEN YOU CAN'T BEAT THE HEAT

 It happens. The reality is that it's just going to be hot during your briefing and that's all there is to it. However, you are in charge and the realities of the situation need to impose on the reality of your plan. You have an obligation to the information which means you have an obligation to the audience.

Is there anything in your presentation that can rouse emotion or debate? You get the point.

EXPECTATION MANAGEMENT

Heated rooms create heated emotions. A simple spark that could be doused with pinch in any other setting could be an instant inferno in a room full of hot and tired participants.

You must present what you must present, but do so in recognition that you will likely need to mitigate reactions more often and with more assertiveness than normal.

How long is your presentation? When the heat goes up you can expect the normal attention span to diminish with every degree above average room temperature. Consider additional breaks and modify your content to include more audience participation.

Is your topic complex or technical? The only thing better than mathematics and complex problem solving are doing so in the heat...said no one. Once again, you must present what you must present. The show must go on. However, modifying the presentation to only demand high levels of mental energy in as few places as possible is better. Sticking to a script of running one hurdle after another might be warranted, but do not expect it to be effective.

CUT, CUT, CUT!

Remember the example of the Director's cut. When it comes to any effective message or story it is so often the case that less is more. If you and your audience have no choice but to share a common hardship of a hot poorly ventilated event, then do everyone a favor and strip it down to the bare essentials. Even the clever meme or short comedy sketch at the start should hit the editing room floor.

Something that might get belly laughs on a crisp Friday morning will produce sighs, groans, and rolling eyes on a hot Monday afternoon. You are not going to save the day with humor, interesting side notes, and clever conversations starters. All you can really do is shorten the duration of the hardship

WHAT ABOUT YOU?

You may not have actual spotlights (if you do, arrange to have them turned off) but being in the figurative spotlight is its own form of heat. Unless you are a professional, seasoned presenter with material that you know inside and out, you can always expect to feel about one or two degrees warmer than your audience. Even if you start out as one cool customer you may be only one audience comment or question away from a blood pressure spike or shot of anxiety.

Expectation management comes into play again.

Warm equals uncomfortable. Be ready. It's normal.

Wear the coolest outfit or uniform modification that is appropriate and comfortable. Use subdued body language and minimize your motions. Rehearse your presentation and focus on breathing (more about this in later chapters). If your breathing is getting shorter that is a red flag that your emotions are starting to take charge. It is also a signal that you are going to start feeling even warmer in the very near future. In a hot room, such process could go downhill quickly.

Last, but not least. Make certain your hygiene is on point. You need to start as clean, fragrant, and dry as possible. You want a uniform or clothing that still has the lingering scent of soap and softener. If the presentation is in the late afternoon, then consider a quick shirt or top change as well as washing your face just before you hit the stage. Even the psychological factor of these two actions will help you feel in control when you take your place in front.

Time to get real. Is there even a chance that you will have the "classic" wet armpit look?

Think ahead. Either mitigate with clothing choice or plan on keeping arm movements low and subdued.

BOTTOM LINE:

Your first course of action is proactive preparation. Find out what climate to expect, and then do what you can to mitigate any potential problems. If that means you start off with a room that's "freezing" then find out how to make it happen. If you must adapt to a situation you can't control, then consider the previous ideas. Doing nothing and just suffering (while your audience suffers) through the status quo is the only bad choice.

LOGISTICS (GREATEST POTENTIAL FOR DISASTER)

This is where everything you don't know or didn't bother to think about prior to arriving at a new location will show up and embarrass you. Logistics means that you and everything you need to be successful shows up at the right place and the right time and in the right quantity. If you are only human, you frequently fail to plan when you are in your own organization. This is because you don't have to. You already know so much about the environment, that you just rely on the immediate access to necessities and solutions.

- You don't think about the laser pointer, because it is always under the podium or in your desk drawer.

- You don't wonder about the markers because you know they were just replenished last week and there are spare sets in the conference room closet.

- You know which remote does what and which light switches control which light panels.

- You know who to call or grab to fix almost any emergency or shortcoming.

- You know where the printer and copiers are and the peculiar ins and outs of those finicky beasts. You also know where the spare paper and toner is.

- You don't have to plan to arrive, you are just down the hall.

- Your parking space is a given and you will be in your normal work environment and routine prior to start time.

- You work in proximity to the briefing area and generally have a sense of what condition it is in and the configuration of tables and chairs on any given day.

The list could go on, but the point is that you can take nothing for granted when you put your show on the road.

Make a checklist of literally everything you will need for your presentation and realize that if you don't bring it with you, then don't count on having it when you arrive.

NOTE: Many things can be arranged ahead of time and anything to prevent you from carrying a foot locker of material into the facility on the day of event is preferable, however, verify, verify, verify. Put your eyes or hands on materials on site as close to the event as possible and have a back-up plan.

- ✔ Erasable Markers / Permanent Markers

- ✔ Laser Pointer / Wooden Pointer

- ✔ Podium

- ✔ Butcher Block paper / Stand

- ✔ Number of hard copies needed plus ____ extra

- ✔ Presentation forwarded digitally to POC plus extra copy on CD/DVD

- ✔ Required number of tables and chairs are available and arranged

- ✔ Extra Shirt/Top/Pants in case of last minute spill or stains

- ✔ Monitors Screens work and tested

- ✔ Microphone available and ready

- ✔ PA system set to correct volume and dynamics

- ✔ Lights and changes in lighting are understood/rehearsed

- ✔ POCs are tracking the time, requirements, and will be available for last minute issues

- ✔ Personal Business Cards

- ✔ Parking arranged

- ✔ Average travel time at pertinent time of day is rehearsed

- ✔ Other

Another aspect of logistics is the state of the battlefield.

Ever walked into your conference room to discover that an event during the evening prior left your briefing area in veritable ruins? Yes, you can get frustrated, you can find out who is responsible and make sure it never happens again, but it needs to be fixed.

Guess what, those same circumstantial troubles befall every conference room and briefing space in the world. Maybe Murphy has such a plan for the facility you are about to visit. What is your plan to make sure this possibility doesn't cause any problems?

Finally, as always, expect the unexpected. It's not personal, just another day and another opportunity to show your peers that you are bigger than whatever speed bumps land in your path.

PART FOUR: "WHEN"

Either you run the day, or the day runs you.
—Jim Rohn

"WHEN" FAQ'S

1. Is there a "best" time of day to give a briefing?

   a. There are certainly some things to consider. The blocks of time near lunch time or the end of the day lend themselves to an impatient and distracted audience. Then there are days of the week. Monday morning may not be the best time to deep dive into a decision brief.

   b. Almost any block of time on the calendar can present advantages and disadvantages. It is worth your effort to be mindful of this reality when you finalize your presentation.
   See "Time of Day Matters" (Page 100)

2. How can I be prepared for sudden schedule changes that cut my allotted short?

   a. You can find out about schedule changes on short notice. It is not necessarily easy to chop a presentation's content at the last minute. If you have a standard presentation which you are asked to deliver regularly, you should have a short and long version. When you have a condensed or extended version already prepared and ready go, you are always ready for short notice changes.

b. A long version of your presentation also serves as a source of quick grab content or "extra slides" when a tough Q and A session presents itself during your standard brief. It is always good to say, "I actually have that laid out in one of my extra slides..."

See "Time Available—Find Your Template" (Page 96)

See "Time Available—Find Your Template" (Page 96)

TIME AVAILABLE—FIND YOUR TEMPLATE

Thus far, there has been intermittent focus on time available. You may need to take the same presentation that you have provided over a dozen times and condense it to a few minutes of "wave-crest" high-lights. As difficult as that maybe, the greater challenge might be the request to *expand* your current presentation.

While most briefings are once in a lifetime or perhaps twice a year or less. You may be in the business of providing the same material repeatedly, and to varied audiences, under variable circumstances.

If you have one of those frequent presentations, then consider per-fecting three versions. The standard version, the short version, and the enhance version.

The standard version speaks for itself. This is the version that you probably already know, "love," and can almost recite in your sleep. It doesn't need much work, but always appreciates the frequent update and additional reference.

The Short Version

Artists, professionals, and anyone who is invested in their trade is hesitant to shrink their talking points and leave the stage in an expedited fashion. In an earlier section, the concept of editing and directors' cuts was used as a point of thought. However, when it comes to ideas and information you are part performer, part expert, but also part salesperson.

You may or may not be looking to literally sell something, but you are asking your audience to invest their own energy, insight, and priorities into your material. If you didn't want to affect individual or corporate decisions and discussions, then what is your purpose for communicating your information? At the very least, you clearly are asking the audience for their time. As much as everyone takes time for granted, it is the most valuable thing any organization has.

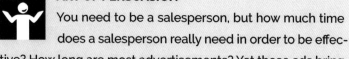

ART OF PERSUASION

You need to be a salesperson, but how much time does a salesperson really need in order to be effective? How long are most advertisements? Yet those ads bring in the millions every day.

Unless you are buying a house or a car, you probably prefer all your interactions with rank and file sales representatives to be as short as possible. Even if it is something as substantial as a house, you really want to get the important details covered up front and quickly. In any case, you probably make up your mind about the product or the representative or both within a few minutes or seconds of interaction.

You may not want to condense your entire presentation into a simple paragraph or even a single discrete statement. However, any good sales pitch is built around just such an idea. It is likely that your presentation is instructional and requires several important concepts and even problem-solving activities to be meaningful. That is alright, if you must condense into a few talking points, then sell the take-away skills and knowledge that your audience can expect if they get your full-length presentation.

If a product representative can convince people to depart with their money with a short statement or a moment of interaction, you too can leave a lasting impression in a short period of time. Create your short-time template, practice it, refine it. Few things are more difficult than perfecting a single pitch line or short interaction. It is an art and you will likely refine your short-version continuously over time.

The Long Version—The Art of the Hidden Slide

Maybe you are the kind who can speak all day on their favorite topic. That doesn't mean anyone wants to hear it. If you are a subject matter expert and have done your research then you can embellish material and add talking points along every point of the presentation. However, what if you were asked to double your briefing time? What would you realistically add that would be meaningful and interesting? How would you still train to standard and not just time?

It is interesting that leaders complain so much about a lack of time to focus on training this, that, or the other, but when extra time presents itself on short notice that extra time is difficult to exploit. Unless, of course, you have a plan.

This could be called the "art of the hidden slide."

Most presentations have slides, charts, graphs, or other materials that are set on the side or simply ready for use if the opportunity presents itself. It is a good practice to have extra slides that embellish your current content. You never know when the VIP in the room will want to delve into one detail or idea in your presentation. Too often, these curious distractions are known to overtake the rest of the allocated briefing time. A presenter with a good set of hidden slides is all too ready to engage in topical 'rabbit trails'.

The hidden slides are also a gold-mine for building the long version of your brief. It goes without saying that you can have as many as you would like on standby, but having them perfected, updated, and rehearsed at all times is something you will thank yourself for many times. If you look at your schedule you probably do not have much time allocated for "add 20 minutes to run time of standard slide deck."

Yet, that is exactly what may happen. If you already have the long version prepped, then you just need to sort, print, and go.

Your other option is to find enhancements. What group activity, test, or discussion do you always wish you had time for? Take a few moments to chart it out as if you were going to present it tomorrow. It will come in handy eventually

Bottom Line: When provided more time, don't just pontificate... Have a plan.

Time of Day Matters

This section is an extension of discussing the impact of climate during your briefing. Time of day will impact several factors pertaining to your audience and this includes the reality that the temperature in the building may vary greatly between morning and evening. Natural lighting to could play an important role in some situations and there is the obvious connection to time of day in that regard.

This is not a book about psychology, but it does not require a PhD to recognize that your attention span, energy, and overall attitude slide from morning to evening. Regardless of when your brief is scheduled consider where you normally are during that time. Look at the battle rhythm for the unit and your own work patterns and consider where your co-workers might really be apart from your briefing.

If a major decision brief is scheduled one hour after yours you can bet that the audience will be looking at you but mentally focused on the next event. Another obvious hazard is placing yourself as the last thing that stands between the audience and the end of the work day...

or even worse, the start of the weekend. More often than not, you have little control over when you conduct a briefing, but if you do, remember that time of day is not necessarily arbitrary.

What about lunch? Not that you would normally schedule an event during lunch unless it was a social one. However, what do you expect to be problems just before or just after lunch? Patience and attention spans wane when stomachs start to growl. The internal alarm clock that tells you that you are supposed to be eating lunch will also tell your brain that the person or thing distracting you needs to go away.

 EXPECTATION MANAGEMENT
So, better to roll right after lunch? Maybe, only now you have the other side of the coin to content with; primarily the sluggishness and lack of energy that people experience after a full meal. It's just a natural fact that the blood that might otherwise go to the brain is hanging around the digestive system to help with the task at hand.

Then again, work is work and as long as everyone is on the clock then you can conduct your briefing when you have to or believe it is best. There is something to be said for pushing through and not worrying about peripheral factors, but time of day is always there for your consideration. At the very least, you will not be surprised by the possible impact of the times you choose.

Here are some questions to consider as you prepare:

1. Is this presentation better suited for the beginning or end of the week?

2. What events come before and after?

3. Will the room need to be re-arranged immediately before or after?

4. Should you make snacks or beverages available?

PART FIVE: "WHY"

Motivation, like hygiene, needs to be refreshed every day.
—Anonymous

BUT WHY ARE <u>YOU</u> DOING IT?

When it comes to work and professional obligations, "why" is pretty straightforward. It's your job. The boss wants it. You need to demonstrate that you are ready for the next job or next promotion. Sometimes, you believe in what you are doing and it is meaningful, but even if it is not, it still needs to get done. So what?

This section is a very brief look at motivation.

It is probably not much of a secret that Americans were drafted to serve in many previous wars. The Korean War was just such a conflict. When you think of being drafted, you probably perceive that a very narrow spectrum of dangerous and unpleasant jobs and missions await you. However, the Army has been able to demonstrate that, like most organizations, it can identify and exploit talent within its ranks.

In 1951, a little known musical prodigy named John Williams was drafted into the Air Force. It should not be surprising that this young man found himself conducting and arranging music for the Air Force Band. Up to that point he merely attended UCLA as a music student and could easily demonstrate exception skill as a piano player. Of course, he would later become the influential composer of movie scores from Jaws to Star Wars and dozens more.

The point is that there is a reason this otherwise anonymous young man was not sent to routine duties and there are reasons you have been trusted with certain responsibilities in your organization. While it is true that duty descriptions are meticulously stated in both doctrine and evaluations, the broad spectrum of "additional duties" and "special taskers" gravitate toward the most able and reliable if not just the most available.

:) **BE YOURSELF**

When you provide briefings or presentations to your own organization or represent your organization in front of varied audiences, you are serving as the face of your leadership and your team as a whole. The degree to which you are successful not only speaks about your own professionalism and competency, but likewise for your section or unit. Not just anyone can deliver a briefing in a way that gives the power players on the team peace of mind.

If you are being trusted to speak to people outside your normal sphere of influence, and no one is there to monitor, assist, or otherwise babysit your performance, then you have demonstrated a valuable skill. There is a reason that YOU are the point of contact.

Perhaps you have a world class poker face, but most of us wear our motivation and personal stake in the unit's mission on our sleeve. You will likely project your feelings about the content of your brief whether you like it or not. Motivation can be an integral part of every presentation.

Since your enthusiasm or lack thereof will ultimately shine through, then if nothing else, take stock in the fact you are seen with high regard within your unit or section. Otherwise, just appreciate the fact that if you do well, you will take that step that begins to separate you from your peers and change the course of your career.

6

PART SIX: "HOW"

Synthesizing the Five W's

*It is common sense to take a method and try it. If it fails,
admit it frankly and try another. But above all, try something.*
—Franklin D. Roosevelt

"HOW" FAQ'S

1. After my first presentation, my supervisor my speaking style was unsteady. I don't remember anything going wrong. What am I missing?

    a. Almost all of your speaking is in the context of conversations. People pause, fish for words, use "uhm… like… so" far more often than they realize. No one notices, unless they hear it in the context of a presentation. Things that work in conversation do not work in front of a crowd. It takes practice, but almost everyone has to break bad habits to be an effective speaker.

    b. Try to focus on speaking a little slower, almost too slow, and you might be surprised at the results…
    See "Know your Speaking Habits" (Page 115) and "Effective Rehearsal" (Page 141)

2. I've heard that I should try to get away from putting everything on PowerPoint. What is the best way to present my information?

   a. PowerPoint is an effective and highly dynamic way to bring a multitude of visual and audio effects together. One guiding principle might be simply, less is more. Fewer slides and visually streamlined slides are going to go over better with an audience than a 150 slide presentation loaded with graphics and tiny text.

   b. If you can present your information by way of question and answer or demonstration, then you can count on a more engaging experience. If you are comfortable in front of a crowd, then learn to cut slides and add audience interaction.
   See "Visual Media" (Page 129)

3. What is a good way to start a presentation?

   a. You are probably looking for what is called an anticipatory set. This is basically a story, a meme, a video, or quote that uses a bit of entertainment to introduce the topic.

   b. If you cannot find a video clip or inspirational quote, the best way to start is with one or two questions. Lean toward "the" question. What is the main thing you want your audience to learn? Turn that into a question which you ask at the start, and then revisit the same question at the close.
   See "Curiosity and the Anticipatory Set" (Page 135)

KNOW YOURSELF

You're the hero of your story but also your own worst enemy. Unless you are honest about your strengths and weaknesses. Maybe it is easy to be honest about your strengths, but there is always the tendency to overestimate. The real trick is knowing how to reconcile a weakness. Your skill set is not perfect because no one is quite that good. But people who know how to build systems and habits that overcome shortcomings can appear to be that good.

With today's technology, there is literally no reason to let a weakness spoil the show. Essentially, there is either an app or a device to manage whatever ails you. Whether it is something on your wrist that reminds you to leave your desk and get in 1000 steps, a set of pushups, etc. or an app that sends any number of personal or professional reminders to your cell phone, there is something out there designed to help you succeed.

So, what kind of planner are you?

Do you come up with great concepts and overarching structure but get lost in putting the details together? Maybe the tiny details are your forte. Maybe you are a little of both. Since a briefing or presentation is essentially the execution of a plan you should recognize where you might have a blind spot.

Even though there is often an app to meet your needs, the human resource is still the best. You know the strengths and areas of expertise amongst your co-workers so when you suspect that a portion of your plan or presentation is missing something that you can't quite put your finger on, it is time to bring that alternate point of view. You might be surprised at how quickly someone else can diagnose a problem or spot an error that you missed.

Can you handle criticism?

ART OF PERSUASION
It really doesn't matter what kind of help anyone around you might offer if you are overly sensitive to what they find. If people know you can't handle the truth they will not give it to you. The good news is, you will blissfully unaware of shortcomings in your products and hold yourself in high regard. The bad news is, everyone else is fully aware.

Anytime you hand a presentation or product to a co-worker for review and critique, expect to be surprised. You can take or leave their comments, but if they see something in a certain way, then you can bet a good portion of your audience will see it as well. Just ask yourself, is this presentation about you, or is it about maximizing the audience's ability to understand?

If you can remove your emotions from the equation and take suggestions and otherwise negative input as a legitimate check on reality, not only will you produce better products, but people will see you as a level headed professional. Better than that. You will actually BE a level headed professional.

Good. Now that we are ready to be honest...

WHAT ARE YOUR PREPARATION HABITS?

Do you procrastinate? Do you handle some things promptly and procrastinate with others?

Think about the answer to those questions and look at the tasks associated with a successful briefing. Which of the following are you likely to take care of immediately, and which one are you likely to, "take care of later?"

- ✔ Prepare Slideshow
- ✔ Update Resource Slides after checking publication dates and sources
- ✔ Rehearse Entire Presentation
- ✔ Memorize key points and definitions
- ✔ Rehearse in front of a peer or target audience member
- ✔ Contact POC to reserve space or confirm time
- ✔ Contact POC to arrange or confirm set-up requirements
- ✔ Check briefing area for equipment functionality and supplies on hand
- ✔ Research latest information on topic
- ✔ Revise notes
- ✔ Print Copies
- ✔ Coordinate POCs to assist with lights/audio/setup/environmental control
- ✔ Reserve enablers (VTC bandwidth, teleconference line reservations, audio/visual, podiums, etc.)
- ✔ Print off large display items (usually requested through installation activity or purchased via commercial source)
- ✔ Arrange coffee, drinks, or snacks

The list is not at all inclusive and probably includes a few completely irrelevant points for your situation, but that is not the point. This should allow you to see the types of tasks that you prefer to handle ASAP versus others.

This could be revealing of your overall tendency to be introverted or extroverted. If you have a natural instinct or dynamic team building and one on one interactions, then you might gravitate toward contacting POCs, rehearsing in front of peers, and solidifying the details of the venue, set-up, and all enablers. If you are more introverted you probably gravitate toward the more academic tasks at hand such as updated content, slides, and research.

Keep all that in mind for the next portion.

Here is a slightly different exercise. Look at the same list and put a number each item that represents the priority of the item, i.e. first to last in terms of priority?

- ☐ Prepare Slideshow
- ☐ Update Resource Slides after checking publication dates and sources
- ☐ Rehearse Entire Presentation
- ☐ Memorize key points and definitions
- ☐ Rehearse in front of a peer or target audience member
- ☐ Contact POC to reserve space or confirm time
- ☐ Contact POC to arrange or confirm set-up requirements
- ☐ Check briefing area for equipment functionality and supplies on hand
- ☐ Research latest information on topic
- ☐ Revise notes
- ☐ Print Copies
- ☐ Coordinate POCs to assist with lights/audio/setup/environmental control

- [ ] Reserve enablers (VTC bandwidth, teleconference line reservations, audio/visual, podiums, etc.)
- [ ] Print off large display items (usually requested through installation activity or purchased via commercial source)
- [ ] Arrange coffee, drinks, or snacks

Is there a difference between those tasks which you know should be accomplished first and the tasks that want to get done before the others? Where are the greatest disparities? For example, the introvert might know that coordinating equipment and facilities as soon as possible is a priority but still naturally gravitates to the academic tasks at hand. An extrovert might focus so much on presentation skill and charisma that updating content is almost forgotten.

For now, let's call the difference between what you know is a priority and what you want to make a priority "risk." It is a risk because you are self-aware enough to appreciate that, left to your own devices, you could fail.

When a risk is identified it should be mitigated by a control mechanism.

The easiest control is a reminder set on your phone or computer desk-top application. You probably don't have to remind yourself to complete your most preferred tasks by a certain date, however, if you know that a task that steps out of your comfort zone needs to be done No Later Than a certain date, then set up the reminders to make sure you don't fail.

Look out for friction.

You set up a reminder to call a POC for audio/visual set-up. Your calendar pings you via your phone and you call. Now you are good to go. Wait, how often does that actually happen? You are going to call, and they will not be in, or they will be on leave, or their phone will just ring, or they will not respond to an email. The possible shortfalls are countless.

BE YOURSELF

Or, in this case, know yourself and work with who you are. If you already have a tendency to avoid a certain type of task, then expect friction to set you back even further. Whereas the logical course of action might be to immediately make another phone call to someone else in the organization, you might be tempted to wait until tomorrow.

Reminders should not be set at the deadline, but well ahead of the deadline. You can expect everything to take longer than expected and that friction is around every corner. Almost nothing is as easy as making a phone call to the listed POC and checking off the requirements.

We almost always know what right looks like in terms of priority and behavior but internal motivations and personal preferences often override. Rationalizing the difference is practically second nature. Otherwise, most Americans would be physically and fiscally fit and hold advanced degrees in the areas of their passions.

After all, becoming physically fit is not rocket science, but actually getting after it is the challenge. Some people are natural born athletes and find that any physical task or habit is easy to engage. The logic and habits of fitness will always seem second nature and easy to incorporate into their daily routines. However, other aspects of a fulfilling and successful lifestyle might require mentorship from a friend.

Once you identify the ups and downs of your own preparation habits do whatever is most effective to overcome weaknesses. New habits, reminders, and even accountability partners are all worth a try.

Know your Speaking Habits

"So uhm, if you look at this graph you will note a vast improvement over last year. Uhm, this is probably sustainable but, so uhm, we have to be careful not be too optimistic. So, uhm, the bottom line is..."

The above passage might look ridiculous in print, but it is not unusual in the course of how people communicate throughout the day. Maybe you have sat through many presentations that sounded like this example, or even worse. After twenty minutes, half an hour, or even longer, it would probably be almost impossible for you to pay attention to the presentation since you would be stuck on the "so, uhm," mannerisms of the speaker.

The interesting, if not unbelievable thing about this situation, is that if the presenter above was provided with evaluation sheets that consistently said, "the speaker needs start sentences with 'uhm,' and 'so, uhm' less often, they would likely act completely surprised. More often than not, our own idiosyncrasies and mannerisms are transparent to us.

The real question is, once you are made aware of a distracting or ineffective habit, will you listen and adapt, or just stubbornly think the critique is invalid and move on?

To start with, you can be sure that you use filler words and expressions in your daily speech and presentations. This is because your brain is involved in synthesis, information recall, and making judgement calls on the best phrases and answers. The more questions or pressure you feel, the more you brain will labor at these tasks. Your brain wants extra time and simplification. It will find both in the form of filler sounds, "uhm" and repetitive words, "so"

What are the most logical ways to minimize the problem?

1. **Rehearsals.** The more you rehearse your content and develop those exact phrases that you are most comfortable and confident in, the less your brain will have to work during a presentation. Muscle memory is preferable to living in problem solving mode in front of an audience.

2. **Inviting Feedback.** Start with a close co-worker and they will likely provide suggestions without any blunt or sharp edges. After this, bring in a supervisor or less "friendly" co-worker. You can expect additional suggestions and a few uncomfortable moments. At some point, you should implement an opportunity for some of all of your audience to provide written, anonymous feedback. That can be very interesting and ultimately taken with a grain of salt. However, you are likely to learn things in this format that you cannot learn by any other method. It's not just about fixing your shortcomings. You also want to maximize your message.

What about those words and phrases that are perfectly suitable and expressive, but overused? For example, there is nothing wrong with answering a comment from the audience with, "Precisely, this is why..." But what if you answer EVERY comment from the audience with "Precisely..."?

By the time you are twenty minutes in, you will experience everything from snickering/whispers to outright trolling in the form of extra comments that provoke you to use, "precisely" just one more time.

What a great way to spend your time in the spotlight. Not really.

The next time you have to provide your supervisor with information or answer questions, deliberately note your own mannerisms. This is the sort of setting that demonstrates your speaking habits at times when your brain is in high gear. Check which sounds, body motions, and words you lean on most when you need a second to put your thoughts together. You can bet that when you brief, you will do the same things.

Speaking of body motions, you might have heard that a certain percentage of communication is non-verbal. How about this, ever misunderstood an email or found out someone had a negative reaction to an email you thought was friendly and helpful? That is because the communication was lacking voice tones, facial expressions, and gestures. When you write any form of communication you take the tone of voice you have in mind for granted.

"Sure, that's a great idea."

Is that sentence affirming, or sarcastic? Both sides are debatable, but without context or other non-verbal clues, the debate could never be resolved.

The bottom line is that you also have facial expressions, melodic patterns, gestures, and other body language that you take for granted but may become equally distracting to an audience. If you are brave enough, you should seek honest feedback on these dynamics as well.

Know your Personality

Consider your own go-to personal qualities that allow you to be successful in your profession and influence your choices of friends and hobbies. Maybe you pride yourself in various attributes, or friends and family remind you about the qualities that make you stand out. Highlight or underline three of the following words that describe you best?

- Friendly
- Serious
- Funny
- Spontaneous
- Procrastination
- Diligent
- Strict
- Disciplined
- Intelligent
- Empathetic
- Quiet
- Articulate
- Organized
- Playful
- Stoic

Note: Those are mostly just the more positive ones.

Look at the keywords that describe you and ask yourself what you would expect from yourself as a presenter compared to someone with opposing qualities. It could be argued that an articulate, intelligent, and organized personality might make the best presenter, but in reality, preparation, rehearsal, and attention to detail will transform any personality into an effective presentation guru.

BE YOURSELF

Avoid adjusting your personality traits to fit the duty description. The goal is to be yourself while recognizing the advantages and disadvantages you bring to the table.

Maybe you are a procrastinator. If you are honest enough to recognize it, then you are ready to put controls in place that prevent you from waiting too long.

Maybe you fumble for words when you are in the spotlight. This means you could plan more rehearsal or memorization time between now and the briefing.

Are you articulate and quick on your feet? The danger might be that you undervalue rehearsing and memorizing key points. Don't let a strength turn into a self-created trap.

Are you known for your wit and generally keep people around you chuckling throughout the day? You can probably rely on that to add life and natural life to your presentations. However... Either the content of the brief or the audience are opposed to quips, jokes, and clever asides. How to you plan to keep yourself in check?

Another hazard associated with a natural sense of humor is learned daily survival mechanisms. For example, assertive people bulldoze their way through life's tough spots. Intelligent people think their way around problems. Charming people schmooze the powers that be.

Humorous people cut tension and conflict with laughter. Put a comedian in a tight spot and they will surprise you will a laugh worthy take on their situation. Most people like that. It can be very effective at skimming over other glaring shortcomings. Can you think of a place where it is not only unhelpful, but might make things worse?

How about the middle of a Q and A with a visibly serious VIP asking some in depth questions? This is exactly the place where charming or humorous personalities like to shine. Conflict, anger, and leaning half-over on their back foot is where they like to interject a game changing comment. In the context of a briefing, the results are likely to be undesirable.

No matter what your humorous instincts are, when you are front and center you should check yourself if you find that your mind is running that direction in a pinch. There is simply no substitute for knowing your topic or being candid about what you don't know. As much as other participants in the briefing appreciate levity, they also appreciate concise responses that keep the presentation moving and the boss on an even keel.

You might be able to see where an honest appraisal of your personality traits and tendencies can be a very valuable way to approach both the planning and execution of a briefing.

You may not necessarily have strengths and weaknesses, just simply a set of unique qualities that can be managed or leveraged to maximum effect.

What Performer Matches Your Personality? How do they work the room?

This section is a short sequel to the previous one.

Who is your favorite actor, musician, comedian, sports personality, or even fictional character? Would you say that you feel you have much in common with that person? Maybe they represent something you would like to be. For the moment, think of someone in these categories that you believe reminds you of yourself and how you interact with others.

For the most part, the person or persons you visualize are successful people. With the exception of a fictional character, celebrities and cultural icons have risen above hundreds or thousands of competing personalities, professional pitfalls, personal weakness, mistakes, etc. in order to stand near the top of the collective heap. It's not necessarily that "if they can do it, then you can do it," but they know how to leverage their personality to great effect in a multitude of situations.

Thanks to the power of the internet you do not have to work hard to find any number of items pertaining to a celebrity.

Try looking up interview video segments in daytime settings, late night satire settings, etc. Seeing these individuals interact with as many other personalities as possible can be interesting. Despite fame and fortune, some people remain quiet and shy. Others can surprise even their biggest fans with calmness, poise, and intelligence.

What makes these scenarios interesting is that people in the inter-view setting are actually working hard. They are invariably jockeying for more words, more camera time, more control of the conversation, self-protection, vindication, saving face, etc. and all with the knowledge that they must choose their words carefully. Any number of mistakes, insults, or slips can alter careers in a heartbeat.

The setting is usually live, the spotlights are real, and all eyes are fo-cused on them. How do they do? How do they handle tough spots? How do the interviewers leverage their own personality to bridge gaps, move conversations, and diffuse issues?

It might seem a little ridiculous at first to watch these events critically, because we take for granted how difficult the interview setting really is. But when were you ever interviewed, for anything, that didn't result in you replaying the scene in your mind afterward and wondering if you did okay?

The modern media interview format allows you to see real pros at work with real scrutiny around each comment and facial expression.

If you have a role model, then take a moment to see how they handle themselves.

HOW

CREATIVITY, INNOVATION, DRY FACTS, LIVELY CONTENT, ETC. ARE ALL GOOD AND ALL BAD

Too often we create false binaries where they are not necessary. It is easy to look at anything and develop an "either, or" mentality. In other words, things are either good or bad, or at the very least, people tend to think so at any given time.

Try this one. Which is better, lively content or a straight presentation of dry facts? Of course, it is a false binary. The simple answer is, "yes." Because it depends, right?

This is where you must deliberately think of what "right looks like" for your situation. If you know that the audience wants a concise, dry presentation, but you also know that you are humorous and have lots of content that is lively and somewhat entertaining, then you know you have a conflict at the outset.

The answers to these questions will be driven by the audience in most situations. You only fail if you fail to meet their expectations or requirements. That is to say, the customer is usually right. However, use your judgement. If you believe that a little variety will be acceptable and genuinely add to the intelligibility of what you are doing, then strike the balance.

Just because creativity is not held in high regard in a certain setting does not mean that it is not needed. Dry facts can either put people to sleep or present themselves in such a way that keeps their attention. Even a humorless briefing needs some innovation and creativity.

Here are some dry but compelling facts from fbi.gov.

- Since 1996 the violent crime rate has decreased from 636 incidents per 100,000 people to 372 incidents per 100,000.

- In 1996 the population of the United States was 265 million. In 2015, the population was 321 million.

- There was a decrease every year since 1996 except for the years 2005, 2006, 2012, and 2015. In those years there was a small increase averaging .2 percent.

- These numbers include rape, a crime that received a revised federal definition in 2013. The new definition qualified a broader range of assault as rape.

- Data is still maintained on the statistical occurrence of rape under the legacy definition.

- The robbery rate has decreased the most dramatically by coming down by as much as half, from 201.9 (1996) to 101.9 (2015).

There is very little room for any humor pertaining to these facts, but creativity is still important. Even glancing at these bullet points you can probably sense the trends and see a lot of potential for discussion, debate, and further analysis.

Look at the first two bullet points again.

- Since 1996 the violent crime rate has decreased from 636 incidents per 100,000 people to 372 incidents per 100,000.

- In 1996 the population of the United States was 265 million. In 2015, the population was 321 million.

If an audience saw that on a slide they could easily absorb the material and might start to think about it. However, anyone who was starting to think about their after work routine or sending a text message under the table might not get so much out of it. No matter how concise or interesting the data is, you still have to read, contemplate numbers, time, and contemplate the relationships while listening to the speaker's comments and shifting focus from the last slide.

So, this is okay.

Changing Crime Rates in the United States

- Since 1996 the violent crime rate has decreased from 636 incidents per 100,000 people to 372 incidents per 100,000 people

- In 1996 the population of the United States was 265 million. In 2015, the population was 321.

Source: fbi.gov

But this might be better.

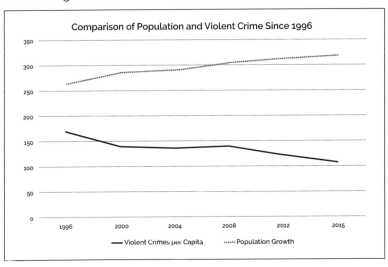

It is a boring graphic, but even someone who is looking at their cell-phone might glance up and quickly decide that those two contrasting trends are interesting. In this case. Graphs have the additional benefit of reducing focus on you and cutting down the amount you need to speak.

The first slide might prompt you to say something along the lines of, "If you read those two bullet points you might note that population as steadily increased as violent crime has been on the decline." Not only is that single sentence, or most variants of it, a bit of a mouthful but it has two disadvantages. One, it keeps the focus of the presentation on you and your performance and two, you need to insert spoken words while your audience is trying to read.

This brings up a general rule. If your chart is text, or bullet-point heavy, then try not to speak for a few seconds after the slide appears. People can process an image or graphic while listening to a speaker, but written words and spoken words at the same time is like listening to different tracks in each headphone piece.

A quick graphic is always preferable because it allows people to see relationships quickly. This spares the time and effort to internally translate data into visualization.

Anytime a picture can replace words (barring any objection from your instructions or supervisor) is good.

Of course, there are infinite "gee-whiz" options to enhance the effect.

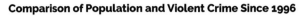

Comparison of Population and Violent Crime Since 1996

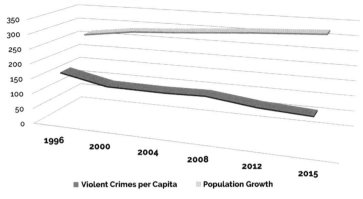

■ Violent Crimes per Capita   Population Growth

The art of finding the perfect intersection of pertinent facts and visualization will hinge on your creativity, experience, and intent of the briefing.

Speaking of intent...

Here is the data again.

- Since 1996 the violent crime rate has decreased from 636 incidents per 100,000 people to 372 incidents per 100,000.

- In 1996 the population of the United States was 265 million. In 2015, the population was 321 million.

- There was a decrease every year since 1996 except for the years 2005, 2006, 2012, and 2015. In those years there was a small increase averaging .2 percent.

- These numbers include rape, a crime that received a revised federal definition in 2013. The new definition qualified a broader range of assault as rape.

- Data is still maintained on the statistical occurrence of rape under the legacy definition.

- The robbery rate has decreased the most dramatically by coming down by as much as half, from 201.9 (1996) to 101.9 (2015).

HOW

How would prepare a chart for the following different purposes?

- An auditorium sized audience receiving a briefing the new federal definition of rape and number of reported incidents
- A panel discussion of violent crime during and immediately after presidential election years
- A working group analyzing statistical links between sexually based crimes and violent crimes overall

Only some of the data applies to each and different charts types and data ranges can tell very different stories when presented visually. Experiment with different chart types until you find the one that says the most in the least amount of time.

Another important question is, what information or graphics would you prepare on a hidden slide(s) in case an in-depth discussion or detailed questions followed your presentation?

Who is your audience? What is the intent of the presentation? What is the topic? How much time do you have?

The answers to those questions determine what right looks like in terms of boring, animated, graphic, photo, text or other choices. You might be the star of the show, but the information should always be the focus of the audience's attention.

VISUAL MEDIA

To PowerPoint or not to PowerPoint? Of course, you *will* PowerPoint. The use of PowerPoint is so universal and so pervasive that PowerPoint itself is now listed as common noun in the English vernacular alongside Kleenex, Post-it and Play-Doh. Even the people who say they hate it, use it, and are generally really good at making presentations with it. What can you do?

First of all, you should become very proficient with any visual medium you use on a regular basis. Whether that means becoming a keyboard shortcut guru and all-around slide-making machine, or simply knowing how to change a projector lightbulb in under five minutes. If your reputation and presentation hinges on a routinely used program or item, then it behooves you to become an expert.

It is no secret that the visual medium is the most powerful and preferred way of transferring information or ideas. PowerPoint gives a presenter an efficient and accessible way to put almost anything in front of an audience's eyes. Of course, nothing can really replace the real thing. How does a photo of an aircraft carrier compare to standing near one while at dock?

Like it or not, *you* are the primary visual. Not only are you three dimensional and physically sharing the same general space as your audience, but the human element is the most powerful. Your facial expressions, gestures, personal hygiene, etc. will have more impact on any presentation than your choice of graphs or themes.

Have you ever noticed that an effective sales person is well groomed, well dressed, poised, and armed with a smile? The product itself will always be secondary to the human interaction between the product representative and the customer. A negative human interaction will turn a customer away from even the most desired product.

Take care of your appearance. Especially in the military. Whereas hair-styles, jewelry, make-up, etc. may fit into a broad range of acceptable tastes and preferences in the civilian world, the military standards are locked in tight. The audience is fully aware of what falls outside the left or right limits and aren't interested in being instructed by a "ragbag" Soldier.

Even a great presentation might be forgotten in a few days, but the memory of a sloppy presenter will endure. A tight haircut/style, fresh and unwrinkled uniform top, properly bloused boots, all patches and particulars in order are all non-negotiable.

Of course, the human element is also the use of the voice. There will be more about his later, but for now, consider your words as part of a performance and like any actor, choose facial expressions and body language that drives your words home.

> *You may write me down in history*
> *With your bitter, twisted lies,*
> *You may tread me in the very dirt*
> *But still, like dust, I'll rise...*
>
> *—Maya Angelou*

Look at this example of a way in which the human element is superior to any other visual medium. There are two presenters and each of them want to start their presentation with a passage from a famous poem. The first one places the poetry on the screen and gives the chart a moment of silent meditation to take it in.

An unexpected moment of silence and poignant text are effective and make an impression, but there might be a better way.

 ART OF PERSUASION
The second presenter simply stood solemnly and confidently before the audience and, with a voice that was almost too soft, said,

"Before we engage in today's topic, I think it might be relevant to consider these words from Maya Angelou's powerful poem, Still I Rise. (pause and fix gaze forward) 'You may write me down in history with your bitter, twisted lies. You may tread me in the very dirt but still, like dust, I rise.'"

This delivery takes something that is already poignant and makes it very personal. There is something about hearing anyone recite a poem, verse, or passage from memory. The first presenter would demonstrate that they know how to set a tone, but the second presenter would establish a personal connection with the audience.

Don't be afraid to add a dash of theater. However, in most cases, only a dash.

Bottom Line: PowerPoint is powerful, but somethings are best delivered without a slide. Mix things up.

OBJECTS AND DEMONSTRATIONS

People love visuals, but hands-on is the best. A video of a new type of tank round is always a hit, but can you get them out to the range? What about a 1:1 scale dummy for display?

Any type of relevant object that audience members can pass around and examine during your presentation will bring them in. Even something as mundane as a relic ID Card inside a protective sleeve will have audience members anticipating their chance to handle and examine the item. Do you want to talk about a new piece of personal tactical gear and how lightweight it is? Soldiers know how much individual tactical items weigh. As soon as they feel the difference for themselves, you won't need to say another word.

Demonstrations can be a little more tricky. Most topics probably involve a website or program that the audience is either learning to use or encouraged to try. A frame by frame how-to with circles and arrows is good, but clicking through the site or software is better. Of course, the risk is the fact that Murphy will want to strangle your bandwidth or router at that exact moment.

For a reliable demonstration of a program or website, consider creating a screen-capture video snipped from an actual session or system access. You can embed the video and always know that the visual experience will be identical and ideal.

CONSIDER AN ASSISTANT

Some demonstrations require assistance. There is an old magician's technique that involves bringing a volunteer to the stage in order to assist. Of course, the "volunteer" is actually in on the trick and helps pull it off. There are plenty of times when your topic might be enhanced by some controlled audience interaction. If you carefully plan and rehearse an interaction or moment with an accomplice ahead of time, you can really get the audience engaged.

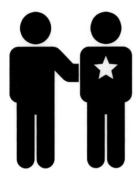

It could be something light-hearted such as introducing a new uniform policy change.

Briefer: "I'm sorry everyone, we have to pause for a second. We have a PFC in the audience who thinks he can wear whatever shirt he wants under his uniform top. (points at Soldier and then pulls on own shirt for emphasis) Hey! Get with the program."

Accomplice: "Roger, Sergeant, chapter five, paragraph 36c."

Briefer: "Excuse me? (pulls up pertinent text on the screen that demonstrates that it is now ok to wear that t-shirt) Oh, well, there you go. Carry on, Soldier."

Of course, everyone will know it was staged and get a good chuckle, but it is a good way to highlight that fact that some changes are unexpected as well as the embarrassing consequences that await any leader who doesn't know the latest standards.

Caution:

Having an accomplice makes some things possible that would otherwise never happen, such as showing disrespect or hurling an insult to or from the stage. This is territory that will get everyone's attention in a big way, but you better make certain the leadership gives input and agrees that the problem being addressed is serious enough to warrant messing with the audience's real emotions.

COMMO CHECK

Gremlins are real. Any system, electronic device, machine, connection, etc. has an uncanny tendency to work all the time except the most important time.

 RESEARCH ALWAYS PAYS
You may want to check any and all systems, microphones, speakers, lights, monitors, projectors, remotes, and laser pointers the day before a presentation. Most major problems can be fixed or adapted to on 24 hours' notice. However, today is always a new day. Everything that you checked yesterday and then put under lock and key until today has the potential to surprise. Don't forget to check one or two hours ahead of the event and then again about 20 minutes out.

There will still be the occasional surprise but heaven helps those who help themselves and gremlins prefer lazy caretakers.

LESS IS MORE (SLIDES, CHARTS, AND EVERYTHING ELSE)

This is not the first mention of the 'less is more' concept in this book and may not be the last. A section on visuals warrants a reminder. You will inherit presentations and build your own. You will hear that the boss loves this presentation or that presentation the way it is. You will take some pride in your own creation. You will seek ways to make more slides and charts minimize your burden during a presentation.

Those are all good things, but the hazard is excess. People like something and that becomes the reason it stays. The effectiveness or necessity is no longer questioned. You should always find ways to use the tools of the trade to make your job easier, but when do you cross the line of increasing your own comfort at the expense of the audience?

But since a picture is worth a thousand words, here is one for your consideration.

Comparison of Population and Violent Crime Since 1996

- Since 1996 the violent crime rater has decrease from 636 incidents per 100,000 people to 372 incidents per 100,000.

- In 1996 the population of the United States was 265 million. In 2015, the population was 321 million.

- There was a decrease every year since 1996 except for the years 2005, 2006, 2012, and 2015. In those years there was a small increase averaging .2 percent.

- The numbers include rape, a crime that received a revised federal definition in 2013.

Why do think that population and the icidence of crime have an inverse relationship?

CRIME SCENE DO NOT CROSS

Comparison of Population and Violent Crime Since 1996

1996   2000   2004   2008   2012   2015

350
300
250
200
150
100
50
0

■ Violent Crimes per Capita   ■ Population Growth

Any Questions?

CURIOSITY AND THE ANTICIPATORY SET

The anticipatory set is a standard aspect of professional instruction. It is so common you likely employ it naturally during your presentations whether you've been told about it or not. An anticipatory set is a short, but topically relevant activity, story, or movie clip/meme that gets everyone's attention, entertains, and prepares them for the upcoming content. "Entertain" might be a strong word. At the very least, it should pique curiosity.

When it comes to the anticipatory set, the chemistry teacher is the envy of the school system. As soon as the bell rings and the students are seated, simply pour one test tube full of mystery liquid into a flask, then add a mystery solid, then wait for smoking, freezing, flaming, flashing, or popping results. Then add, "Today, we're going to find out why that happened..."

Well worth the occasional hazmat evacuation drill.

The anticipatory set is standard practice because it works. An audience brings whatever they were preoccupied with prior to the presentation along with them. They will stay mentally fixated on those issues and actively day-dream or plan the rest of their day during your presentation. Their brains are stuck on watching that channel. The anticipatory set is a just a way to get them to change that channel and tune into you.

However, don't worry about coming up with a gimmick or spend all day coming files for a good video flick or compelling story. The most efficient anticipatory set is just a simple question. In particular, a question that no one likely knows the answer to, but will be revealed at some point during the presentation?

For Example:

"How many people in the United States will go without food today?"

"How much more/less did the United States spend on defense last year than ten years ago?"

"Which college has produced the most Astronauts?"

"Name three famous authors who attended West Point."

"What Army unit was Jimi Hendrix in?" (Someone always know this one—101st Airborne)

HOW

ART OF PERSUASION
It is better to provide a moment of curiosity with delayed gratification i.e. waiting until the mid-point of the brief to see the answer, than something clever with a quick payoff.

"Mary's father has four daughters, Lisa, Leia, Lucy, and...who is the fourth daughter?"

Of course, the fourth daughter is Mary, but there are tons of these types of "are you paying attention to detail" type of trick questions out there. They are fun and good for a quick chuckle at the end of a break, but linking any extra material to your content and drawing out curiosity is preferable.

SUSTAINED CURIOSITY

Sustaining an audience's curiosity has already been alluded to in this section. A question with a delayed answer is an easy technique that you can use throughout the presentation.

An easy option is to introduce a question or problem at the start of the presentation and then wait until the very end and revisit the question for the answer, or perhaps the answer has changed because a new way of looking at the problem was introduced. This technique could be called a book-end method and is well suited for briefings with a more persuasive intention.

As an example of a good book-end worthy topic, a chaplain is going to present their overarching mission, programs, and personal passion for what they do with a group of seemingly cynical leaders in the unit.

The opening question is, "Are chaplains an essential part of the leadership team?" At the beginning the question receives a lukewarm response that seems obligingly positive. Then, after 30 minutes of persuasive talking points and discussion the same exact question is posted on the screen. The format and setting alone cause the audience to feel they should see the situation differently now.

HOW

ART OF PERSUASION

The other curiosity method is just a simple question-answer-question technique that might resemble the momentum of a pendulum. You present a question and avoid an immediate answer in lieu of a two to four slide delay. You do not want to over stretch the tension but may be about each quarter of the way you answer a previous question then present a new one.

Questions that challenge perceptions are the best. People have strong beliefs or at least impressions of the political/social fabric around them. If you ask a question such as "don't answer out loud just yet, but do you believe incidents of rape have increased or decreased in the last ten years?" you will immediately see the wheels start to turn. Everyone will be betting themselves they are right and waiting to see the results.

The bottom line is that a well-timed sequence of Q and A can add tension and energy to any briefing.

HOW

CHECK FOR LOADED LANGUAGE

As you rehearse or make final preparations before the presentation you should scan your slides and talking points for potentially loaded words that might derail your message.

The content of your brief may put difficult topics or discussions at the forefront, but controversy and seething tensions are best avoided in an otherwise harmless information brief.

Depending on the latest world events or changes sweeping through doctrine an otherwise innocent word can have unintended consequences. Check out this list of otherwise legitimate, useful words.

— Conservative: "that is a conservative estimate."

— Liberal: "we will apply this in a liberal manner."

— (plus beware of "left" and "right." Perfectly harmless except for potential context issues)

— Religion, religious, irreligious: "While some may religiously stick to these prescribed methods..."

— Privilege: "Losing your ID will result in a temporary loss of privileges"

— Gender: "These briefings will now break into gender specific groups"

You get the idea. Context, necessity, and contemporary moods all play a role. Something that will not bat an eye today may provoke heated debate tomorrow. Review your materials frequently and keep an eye on facial expressions during presentations. If you notice ill-timed knit brows, rolled eyes, mild headshaking, or just shock, then you may have an unintentional or distracting word or phrase in your presentation.

ARE YOU STARTING FROM SCRATCH?

Never re-invent the wheel unless you are specifically asked to do so. Even if you are asked to delete an entire presentation and create an entirely fresh start, there are still much to be gained from "the file drawer"—more recently referred to as the share drive.

The longer a program or product is around the more likely it is to see a pendulum swing of ideas, problems, and solutions. In the military, leadership is inherently short term. The tenure of command is somewhere between one and three years but usually closer to two. Therefore, a program with ten years or more continuity will have seen many personalities pushing it toward success. The deeper you look into the continuity files of a project the more likely you are to see something old that is perfect or almost perfect for the "new" approach.

If you are simply new to the organization and need to create a briefing for a new initiative, policy, or product, you still need to comb through the file drawer in order to see how this organization presents itself and ideas internally and externally.

Do they have stylized slides with hyperlinks and additional graphics that drop in on each click, or are the presentations more Spartan and minimalistic.

Are there several decks with dozens or hundreds of slides, or is the average less than ten?

What are the common themes for titles, font size, frames, use of corner space, distance between slide content and logo, charts, graphs, color, memes, etc. All of these elements speak to the communication culture that you are now a part of. It is probably different in some fundamental way from your previous position or assignment so save yourself the learning curve and research how products are built in you section.

EFFECTIVE REHEARSAL

Practice makes perfect. Not true. Perfect practice makes perfect. All imperfect practice does is create permanent, unhelpful patterns. For example, if you know that you will take a PT test every six months, and you know the standard for a correct push-up, then you are setting yourself for failure by practicing pushups that are incorrect in form. The same principle applies to learning an instrument, new language, sport, etc.

TRAIN TO TIME

Maybe you already had an experience in time shock. There are two varieties. You prepared 30 minutes of material, but then found yourself on the last slide with 20 minutes remaining. Or, you prepared 30 minutes of material and barely hit the half way point when time was up.

How long does it *really* take to complete your presentation if you presented it to nothing but an empty room without distraction, how long would it take? If you don't know the answer to that, then you will stumble during your event.

For reference, think of a speech, since a speech is wall to wall words without interruption. In that context, a speaker will deliver between 100 and 120 words per minute which means that single page, double spaced, 12 font will consume just a handful of minutes.

— How many words are in your presentation?

— How much time do want for Q and A?

— How often does the VIP or audience typically interrupt and ask questions?

— How much silence to you plan to leave between talking points in order to allow the audience to read the content of your slides?

 RESEARCH ALWAYS PAYS
When you rehearse, start a stop watch first. Try to simulate realistic pauses and space for the occasional question or sharpshooter.

What about the last time your briefed or presented this material? Did you feel crunched? Were you stretching topics out to buy time? Did you run out of questions before you ran out of time? Was your pacing even or did you spend too long on the introduction? Which parts need to be expanded based on audience reactions? Which parts need to shrink or be deleted?

Pacing, rhythm, and time appropriation to topic can transform any briefing radically. If you did nothing else except nail the pace of your presentation, you would improve it dramatically. When you have a sense of controlling the time available you have an abiding sense of that the clock is working for you and not the other way around. Few things provide more confidence, which is always in short supply when you stand before an audience.

Train to Standard

Great, you timed your presentation and your content fits comfortably in the allocated time. There is room for flexibility and a few extra questions. The only problem is, you sounded a bit like an auctioneer.

There are two main reasons why presenters may speak too quickly. The first is nervousness. If you are uncomfortable with an activity, then you want it to end. If you get through the talking points, you are done, so fire away. The other reason is the need to get a lot said in a short period of time. Simply speak faster, and you can keep more content.

Then there is a more intangible factor. Time distortion, or the perception of time. Time "slowing down" is a common perception during traumatic events. Car accidents, close calls, combat, etc. can all activate mechanisms that distort the perception of time. Too often, a few moments in the spotlight can have the same effect.

 You may think you are talking at an even pace in front of a crowd, but what they hear may be very different. To see if you are meeting the standard, practice in front of two or more people in your organization. Among other things, ensure they provide feedback on your pacing and speaking rate.

HOW

If you have any issues of any kind with moving too fast or letting your heartrate rise during a presentation try this little trick.

Speak…Slowly

No need to overdo it, but you might be surprised how your perception of "slow" is the audience's perception of "normal." Here are the advantages of devoting some concentration on speaking "slow"

1. You are focusing specifically on your words and talking slightly slower. This combination will decrease verbal mistakes.

2. You are buying your brain small pockets of time to help it manage the complexity of the task at hand.

3. The attention you focus on your verbal pace is attention that might otherwise turn into negative impulses (i.e. is that person angry about what I said? Are people staring at my hair? Do they think I'm doing a bad job? Etc. The stress of standing before an audience tends to magnify the volume of ordinary self-doubt and criticism. Simply giving your brain an active task as a distraction keeps the negative impulses at bay.

Of course, it is possible to talk too slow and few things are stranger than very...slow...delivery. However, a good delivery on stage is slower than normal conversation. The physical space between you and the audience needs to be filled and talking too quickly will muddy your clarity. Microphones and PA systems, if anything, increase the problem. Sound bounces off of all surfaces. The louder your voice, the more likely the sound waves will overlap and compete in the listener's ear. A small bit of extra space between words and sentences can go a long way.

Then there is advantage number 4!

If, for any reason, you to create an emotional peak of your presentation, then you want to use the power of slower speaking.

ART OF PERSUASION

Suppose your presentation is motivational. Suppose you are presenting a series of statistics and accomplishments that demonstrate that your organization is on an upward trajectory and is about to have another great year.

If you maintain an even, slow delivery during your presentation, you can slowly accelerate your pace near the end and easily generate an emotional crescendo...provided, of course, you combine it with the right motivation phrases, tone, and volume. Just think of the well edited action sequence-punch that tends to occur at the end of movies.

It all led up to one adrenalized moment.

Deliberately managing your pace gives you great opportunities to manipulate the energy of your presentation.

Give it a try in front of a rehearsal audience. You may be surprised.

THE POWER OF THE PAUSE

Silence is uncomfortable and almost always bad.

Radio stations are usually wall to wall sound with little space between anything. Television shows are almost as active. Even movies use soundtracks and audio effects to avoid silence in the absence of dialogue. Silent moments are often the turning points of conversations; and those turns are not usually for the better. A witness on the stand during a trial may look less credible if they pause in silence before answering a critical question. People keep televisions, music players and even white noise generators going for almost every moment of the day to avoid silence in the background.

Silence is notable and powerful.

A good speaker or presenter understands the power of silence and learns to absorb a few seconds of discomfort in the silent spotlight in order to acquire a payoff in the delivery. It can be sprinkled throughout or saved for a poignant moment.

Go ahead and pull up a video of any great speaker. The *I Have a Dream* Speech by Martin Luther King is a solid go to. Aside from all the other aspects of mastery that you will hear in such a speech, you will also hear several well placed and powerful pauses. Sometimes there are pauses mid-sentence. But they add up to great effect.

They allow the audience to contemplate and that contemplation adds gravity. They also create a rhythm.

Of course, attempting to imitate anyone is always a bad idea and most presentations are far too mundane to warrant the techniques of inspirational speakers. However, there is almost always a good place to insert a pause or extra second of silence.

"These statistics show a decline in violent crime, but what if...(pause)... what if we compare it to population growth during the same time?"

A question combined with sudden silence always re-centers the attention of the audience. You would likely see people gazing down at their phones or daydreaming tune back in.

Once again, it's always worth a try.

YOU ARE PREPARE TO SPEAK BUT PREPARE TO LISTEN:

You will probably build in a question and answer segment at the end or sprinkle in opportunities for questions throughout. However, questions may emerge at any time. You might have the most challenging question that you are least prepared to answer just after your opening sentences. These are easy ways to get thrown off of your rhythm and out of your comfort zone.

Rehearsing is essential to success and the more you rehearse the more confident and professional you will be; however, rehearsal develops muscle memory. You will practice talking points and get a good rhythm for each slide and major talking point. Each interruption throws your practiced balance off the rails. It can be hard to back on track.

Therefore, train as you fight.

When you rehearse in front of a co-worker or small test audience ask them to throw at least one wrench into the works every so often. Public speaking, and therefore presentations, are necessarily uncomfortable so the desire to stay on point and get your talking points complete can be strong. You don't have to like interruptions and even addressing them just long enough to say, "please save all questions to the end," can cause a problem. However, don't let them see you sweat, and don't let them see you get agitated.

HOW

DURING THE BRIEF

Now it is time to execute the mission.

Before you say a word, just take a moment to center yourself and ensure that you start out relaxed and emotional subdued. Yes, motivated and energetic is good, but anxious and agitated are not. You may not be able to force yourself to be less nervous, but you can appreciate that your body can tell you how you are doing and you can affect how you are doing with your body. What does that mean?

Shoulders. It only takes a second to think about your shoulders. Are they tensed up. Decide to relax and drop your shoulders and see what happens. You were probably more tense than you realized. Your body will give you an indicator of how you are really doing. However, when you deliberately drop and relax your shoulders, you also send a signal to the butterflies in your stomach to calm down.

Step two. Take two or three slow, full breaths in through the nose and out through the mouth. Same principles and effects as the shoulders. If you are nervous at all, then your breathing is going to be faster and shallower than normal. As soon as you break that cycle with a couple of full breaths, you benefit with a more relaxed introduction.

It is customary to introduce yourself at the start of most presentations and fairly standard to briefly describe the agenda. In your workplace, the introduction is not necessary and often times the agenda is practically second nature to the audience. In all other situations, you should **make sure that the audience know who you are and why you are there.**

"Hello, I'm SGT Smith and we are going to look at recent trends pertaining to sexual assault in the Army. Next slide, please"

ART OF PERSUASION

Okay, but do they know who you are and what you will be talking about?

"Hello, I'm SGT Smith and I've spent three years working in the Judge Advocate's office where I frequently assist with cases related to sexual assault. Today's presentation compares incidents of sexual assault in the military to the civilian sector as well as prosecution rates. It sounds like apples to apples comparison at first, but the details are more complicated. Next slide, please."

The second introduction gives the audience a great deal of context about your unique expertise and understanding of the topic. It also establishes some curiosity and sets expectations in a very specific direction. The first introduction would elicit a response akin to, "got it, let's go." The second version might be more like, "Hmm, interesting."

Even though the briefing format is primarily a speaker and an audience. It is still direct communication from person to person. People always like to know who they are, where they stand in relationship to the speaker, and what is really going on.

START LOOKING FOR THE "LIGHTBULB" RIGHT AWAY.

You come prepared with slides, handouts, talking points, additional research, hands-on displays or demonstrations, and maybe even the occasional accomplice. But you usually have at least one or two more assets in the room. Any given group of people will represent a vast array of knowledge and personal/professional experiences. No matter what you are talking about, there is someone out there who has something to contribute or a passion for the topic.

You might only say your name and make a reference to your background and already see one or two faces in the audience light up. It is fairly obvious when you strike a chord with someone. Anytime you see it, if you have time, stop and acknowledge their response.

"Hey, I saw that back there. Do I have some fellow Delta Dogs in the room?"

See what is going on out there. Even if it is best to keep your program moving forward, you can always go back to a reaction at a later time.

Nods, clock glances, knitted brows, crossed arms, and tilted heads are all sure signs that something is happening out there. If the signals don't match your content or your expectation, then it is time to find out what is going on. You don't want to be a mile down the road before you find out you're not just on the wrong track but alienating the audience.

"Okay, now when I first put the statistics about murder rates in the last five years I saw a couple of folks that looked like they had some insight. You still out there?"

Demonstrating that you are paying attention to the audience and keeping a note of what is going on around you will always resonate well and reflect well on your skill as a briefer.

BE READY TO SHIFT GEARS

EXPECTATION MANAGEMENT
You would always think you are ready to be flexible. But are you really expecting to use that flexibility during this presentation? If you are expecting it, then you will not feel off balance when you actually do it.

You've seen enough presentations and classroom instruction to see flexibility done both poorly and well.

Poor flexibility is simply allowing a necessary diversion or jump to turn into a downward spiral of one rabbit trail after another. If you are easily distracted or like to joke that you are "sort of ADHD," then you might find that it is natural, if not fun, to leave the agenda in the dust.

If rabbit trails are your tendency or simply common in this setting, then you may want to designate an accomplice who simply gives you a signal to let you know when it is time to reel it in or check the clock.

Good flexibility, like most things, is a bit of an art. Discernment is key. You do not want to be rigid but you do not want to lose control. Some comments or questions can be easily diverted to the end or an upcoming segment of the brief. Then again, maybe the situation dictates that jumping to the next section early is the best course of action.

After making the decision about indulging impromptu comments and questions is the decision to cut the diversion short or let it run. You have to have a feel for you overall objective. It goes back to the question,

"What are you trying to say?" or what is that bottom line?

If you believe that an unexpected comment or diversion can become an excellent platform to make your point more efficiently, then you may be able to skip a few slides and just let the conversation continue with its own life. Sometimes an audience will signal that they are either more knowledgeable or more eager than you expected. As long as you meet your intent, the exact road to getting there won't matter so much.

The nature of your presentation or the timeframe may dictate that you simply plough through any questions or distractions, but practice responding and redirecting in a courteous manner.

Shifting gears could also be a decision that you make based on your own judgement. Maybe you designed your presentation for your audience and expected certain questions and talking points to resonate or generate a response. If, after a few slides you realize that nothing is hitting home as planned or expected, then be ready to change gears. The facts, stats, charts, and materials won't change. Everything in your deck can be used in a variety of ways. If your gut instinct is to jump onto another path, then go for it.

RESEARCH ALWAYS PAYS
One of the great payouts to research and knowing your topic is gaining almost infinite flexibility.

HUMOR WORKING? GREAT, DON'T PUSH IT.

This topic was introduced early. If humor does not come naturally to you, then just do your thing. An audience will rarely note a lack of humor in a presentation if humor is even acceptable under the circumstances. Adding anything that is both unnecessary and unnatural is a bad idea.

BE YOURSELF
If you can't help but add a little humor or the situation warrants it, then do your thing. If your jokes fall flat, then take the hint. But if you find that your punchlines are hitting home and you start to get on a roll, then look out. One of two things will happen. Either you will start to lose effectiveness and finish your briefing without meeting your goal, or you will leave a bad impression on ranking individuals in the room; probably both.

It is just another instance where you have to know yourself and your own weaknesses. You can't help but get into a natural groove no matter what you are doing. There are times when certain strengths become weaknesses.

Once again, an accomplice in the room can help you with a few signs and signals that let you know when you are crossing a line. The literal and figurative temperature of the room is very different on stage when compared to the audience. An accomplice is your window into the audience's perception and reality.

THE EBB AND FLOW OF ENERGY

Ever see a movie that was wall to wall action? They are few and far between. Despite the fact that people watch movies for great action sequences, they grow stale after a certain amount of time. A good presentation, like a good story, has an ebb and flow of energy.

Even a dry topic deserves better than flat line energy.

In a previous section the emotional power of pacing was discussed. A quite speaking voice and an even pace can vary and move into quicker, louder segments that stimulate a sense of action and variety in the audience. It may sound manipulative to think you can pre-plan emotional responses and energy levels in your brief, but entertainers and writers do it all the time.

 ART OF PERSUASION
There is a reason why musicians will arrange the songs in a certain order. There are songs that are best to open with and songs that should be at the close. What is more, the balance between upbeat and slow songs needs to be right. It is an art and a science and it takes experience to get good at it.

There are plenty of musicians who can tell you, even before they take the stage, when the audience is going to come to their feet, when you will see tears, etc.

You probably don't need to master this art or think too hard about it, but you should rehearse different techniques to get the energy moving in your presentation.

Tone of voice, pace, physical gestures, movement on stage, Q and A vs. narrative, memes vs. text heaving slides, technical/ serious vs. easy to digest, etc.

These, and several others, are your elements to play with. They all convey a certain type of energy and effect on the audience. It will be more fun for both you and them if you find a way to work the variety of options to keep the energy flowing. Any stirring of the water is better than flat.

EYE CONTACT VS. EYE AVERSION

This concept plays back into rehearsal. It is hard to do something physically on stage when it was not previously rehearsed. However, eye contact is most prone to failure when faced with an audience. As a presenter, you already know what wrong looks like pertaining to yourself.

- Eyes fixed on the floor or excessive glances upward
- Eyes buried into index/note cards
- Staying focused on the slides and not looking at the audience
- Staring above the audience or around the audience but not at the audience.
- Always returning to the same one or two audience members when you look out

These mistakes leave variable impressions from unprofessional to just plain creepy.

The mistakes are easy to make. Two variables will drive you into problems. Once again, stage fright and an overworked brain are to blame. It is hard to be zero percent nervous about a presentation, even if you have learned to give that appearance. Those with the rare genetic disorder known as Urbach-Wiethe Disease (literally cannot feel fear) might be the exception.

As you become nervous in front of a crowd, there are two possible impacts on where you place your eyes. The first, and most common, is to simply avoid eye contact. Disengaging the crowd is just a good way to try and forget they are even there and you don't have to worry about their reactions or what they might be thinking. The other pitfall of nervousness is that you will seek a "friendly face." There are friendly faces in every crowd. If you are mid presentation and you realize you looked out to the exact same person for "affirmation" several times, then mix it up.

 The other variable that will draw your eyes around the room in undesired patterns is just the fact that your brain is working hard. Maybe you are familiar with the art of watching body language and know that some believe that people who are about to tell a lie look down before they talk whereas people trying to recall facts look up. Maybe it is true, but you can bet that when your brain is working overtime your eyes get involved.

No matter what the cause there are two solutions; experience and practice. Experience is something you can't control. You either have it, or you need it, or both. Then again, an accomplice/assistant can also come in handy. You can rely on looking out at them more often than others and they can indicate that you need to change it up.

Rehearsal merely requires a technique and a couple of guidelines.

Eye Rehearsal Technique

Try to avoid picking favorites. Instead of gravitating to those friendly faces in the crowd, simply develop a rhythm. When you first look out at the crowd go dead center. Always start in the center. You don't even have to look at one person in particular. You can look at the space between two people. But the next time you look out move to the either the right or left portions of the room.

The keys are variety and duration. No matter where you fix your gaze you should shoot for a three to five second window. You can think, 'look left, look right, look center.' Or perhaps 'noon, three o'clock, six o'clock,' it really doesn't matter. So long as you accomplish variety and a good 3-5 second duration, you are good to go. Practice this. After a while, you will scan the room without thinking.

 ART OF PERSUASION
You can portray the persona of a seasoned professional even if you are a nervous beginner.

1. Do not fixate on the slides or your notes. Spend at least half your time engaging the audience with your eyes. The goal is to get to 100%

2. Avoid fixating on one or two individuals but practice dividing your attention throughout the room.

3. You can look between people to help alleviate stage fright.

Eye contact, or some proximity thereof, is the norm in human communication. You will not connect with your audience if your head is buried in your notes or fixated on the screen. Getting your eyes away from note cards and the video screen won't happen without some deliberate effort on your part.

Work in this area is one of the quickest ways to convince your audience that you know what you are doing and are in control.

SLOGANS AND CATCH PHRASES

If you are using a presentation that plays into slogans or catch phrases they are probably not of your own design. Slogans and catch phrases work their way into any important program or product as a way to sink into the memory of the audience.

For example, when the Army wants to encourage Soldiers know how to intervene and prevent suicide it encourages them to ACT.

- Ask your buddy
  - Ask the question directly: Are you thinking of killing yourself
- Care for your buddy
  - Actively listen to show understanding and produce relief
- Escort your buddy
  - Never leave your buddy alone/escort to chain of command or health care provider.

The topic could not be more serious and so anything that helps a fellow Soldier remember what to do is good. As it turns out, acronyms and slogans work. At the same time, audiences have been acronymed and sloganed to death. Hence, these effective methods of conveying mass memorization have become memes unto themselves and often cause your audience to tune out.

That just means that you need to make sure you maximize the power of the slogan. Even if audiences are sick of them, the acronym and the slogan are still the most effective way to create a lasting message. Even if an audience is making fun of the acronym, they are still demonstrating that they remember it.

ART OF PERSUASION

Your best bet is to be real. Handle your slogan or your acronym in such a way that shows that "you get it." You understand that that your audience has been made as cynical as can be when it comes to slogans. But you are in this together.

Your tone should focus on the importance of the topic and the value of knowing the bottom line versus promoting a slogan as if it were some unique invention. For example.

"I know you are all acronymed to death, but these three letters can help you make the difference in someone else's life."

Keep it real by having fun with it. Every so often, just break and ask something like,

"Someone remind me, what does the "A" stand for?...right. And give me an example of 'asking your buddy.' What does it mean?"

Then later on,

"The 'A' stands for...right. And the 'C' stands for...good. So now, someone read the 'E' for me."

You can transform something as mundane as another acronym or slogan into a group participation event. It can be fun. No matter how cynical the audience is, you can maximize partici-pation and retention.

CONCEPTUALIZATION AND METAPHOR: MAKING COMPLICATED IDEAS SIMPLE

Compare this:

"Maybe people are good, and maybe they are bad. Either way, people will reveal themselves more through deeds than words. The end result is character. If you think about leaders you have worked for, you probably think about their character first, but wasn't that impression made of countless separate actions and decisions? In time, you learned what direction that person would go based on their character. Their conscience was probably more to thank for your memory of them than all their education, experience, and words of wisdom combined"

To this:

"Conscience is a man's compass."
—Vincent Van Gogh

Arguably, the second example says the same thing as the first. However, the second is more concise and more memorable. It is the simplest expression of the intended message.

This is the power of metaphor.

You are probably already using this power in your presentation and just in your daily life in general. Anytime you have the need to express something abstract or complicated to another person it is natural to search for metaphors or comparisons to more familiar concepts.

In the above example, it is more effective to connect the intuitive understanding of a compass with the abstract idea of the conscience. The conclusion is debatable and opinions vary but at least no one is wasting time debating the original premise.

 When you conduct a briefing or presentation you have a lot to think about and manage. You will probably forget much of what you said and did, but you will likely remember audience reactions, difficult questions, and comments. Were there sticky spots where the audience just didn't seem to get it? Did you have to re-phrase or repeat something? Were you asked a question that indicated that one or more of your points just didn't register?

If the answer to any of those questions is yes, you have discovered an area that needs improvement. Looking for a good metaphor or familiar comparison could be the improvement you are looking for.

But wait, your topics are too technical for metaphor and the difficulties are just a necessary evil. Perhaps. An instructional presentation must necessarily get involved in the real rigor and mental efforts worthy of the topic. However, all that brainpower might be more efficient and effective if you can frame the complexity with a good metaphor or working model at the start. People like to wrap their heads around a concept before they dive into the weeds.

Is your topic more complicated than Einstein's theory of relativity? Not likely, but look at this.

First, there is the classic quote from Einstein himself (paraphrased). 'A man who spends an hour speaking with a beautiful woman might think it seemed like a moment, but to place his hand in scalding water for a minute would seem like an hour. That is relativity.'

Of course, there is no substitute for learning the real computations of the theory but, those who begin that journey might find it is easier to get started and stay motivated by thinking of that quote.

Another way to accomplish the same goal of introducing something very complex is introduce the basic problem in a way that people can understand:

"Imagine you are an astronaut in deep space. You look out the capsule window and everything is perfectly dark with no planets or even stars. Then, another space ship suddenly races by your window and disappears as quickly as it came. Now, was that space ship traveling 100 times faster than you, or was it simply standing still as you raced past it? That is the sort of problem that lies at the heart of Einstein's theories and we will explore the implications of that example during the first portion of the lesson."

It is almost impossible to introduce the unfamiliar without anchoring minds into something familiar. Metaphor, analogies, and comparisons allow you to do this. The best part about a good metaphor is that it will take almost no time to present but could save you a lot of time in the long run.

HOW

PERCEPTION VS. REALITY (WHAT'S IMPORTANT AND TURNING THE TABLE):

Reality: You were unable to sleep the night before and now have very little energy.

Perception: You are unmotivated, lacking energy, or don't really care about your topic.

Reality: Just before the briefing you received terrible news about a problem in your family.

Perception: You are distracted, not really engaged with the audience or the briefing, unfriendly, and too short in your answers.

Reality: You are asked to fill in for someone else and conduct a presentation that you are barely familiar with.

Perception: You are unprepared, unorganized, and unknowledgeable.

Of course, many of these perceptions can be mitigated by a simple disclaimer at the start of your briefing, but in many cases, those disclaimers can be perceived as excuses or just unnecessary. So, once again, there will be a gap between perception and reality.

The question will always be, which of the two really matters, perception or reality? The answer is, of course, perception. Reality should matter, but if no one accepts it, what difference does it make?

In the larger issues, of life time may have a way of letting reality speak for itself, but in the context of a one hour or less presentation, time is not on your side.

These talking points really only serve to demonstrate the importance of preparation and presenting yourself in a very deliberate and conscientious way. The greater point is the fact that you can use the gap between perception and reality to your advantage.

ART OF PERSUASION
When you burst a bubble, you engage and energize the audience. Looking out on a crowd to see multiple "wow" or "ah-ha moments" facial expressions is satisfying and encouraging.

Let's go back to the crime statistics from an earlier section. If you are part of a group or community you are innately aware of general perceptions of different issues or events. Most perceptions are rational and often grounded in the bulk of facts, however, there are plenty of perceptions that are just bubbles waiting to be burst. In this case, the perception that population increases equal increases of violent crime has that potential.

"Now, we know that there are a lot of reasons for societal problems such as food or water shortages, crime rates, cost of living, etc. but it stands to reason that as populations become denser in a given area that some problems might start to escalate."

(That makes sense. Continue.)

"For example, the U.S. population is steadily increasing and urban areas have grown in population by over 5% in the last 20 years. Which is why when we look at FBI statistics on violent crime we see..."

Pause...Change slide to graph chart...pause for effect as they read.

"And... Looks like overall crime actually declined during that time."

This is an example of approaching a gap between perception and reality and then setting up a good moment to turn the tables. The alternative might be a display of facts that passively washes over an audience that starts to daydream or follow other distractions.

The easiest guide to finding these opportunities lies in your own preparation process. As you conducted the research or reviewed your information did you have an "ah-ha moment" of your own? If you found something surprising then it is because your perception was altered. Chances are, a good portion of your audience will walk in with the same potential for surprise on that topic.

THE GETTYSBURG ADDRESS AND ATTENTION SPAN

You've probably heard a lot about attention span.

"Adult attention span runs in 15 minute bursts"
"You should take some sort of break every 20 minutes."
"You will lose people after 30 minutes."
"You have about five minutes before you start losing them."
Etc.

There are a handful of credible studies on the topic and you can add your own experience as a student in various settings as well as a participant in countless briefings.

- How long do you normally pay attention before you momentarily drift off?

- How long do you drift off before you re-center on the topic and the speaker?

- What causes you to drift off more often or less often?

- Etc.

As you prepare and execute your briefing simply take a moment to apply empathy. You know what it is like to receive instruction and information and appreciate certain considerations and an energetic, knowledgeable presenter. Even on your best day there are topics that get the best of you after only a few moments.

Be real and make the most of what you have. However, one principle is always a winner: Less is more. A page of philosophy is better as a proverb, and a lengthy petition is better as a metaphor. Most first drafts of novels and screenplay require significant cuts and scene/character deletions. The more you challenge yourself to say as much, if not more, with less, the better you will be.

No matter what, there is a basis in fact for attention span. As much as possible, try toggle back and forth between complex/technical charts and humorous/general ones. The audience needs time to absorb information, decompress their thoughts and questions, as well as "space out" for a moment without missing something critical.

This leads into the Gettysburg Address. Abraham Lincoln's most famous speech is usually regarded as the most famous speech in American History, competing edge to edge with Martin Luther King's *I Have a Dream* . *The Gettysburg Address* clocked in at 272 words and would take most speakers three minutes or less to deliver.

ART OF PERSUASION

Everyone who believes that they require copious time to get their point across (not counting instruction or technical details) should reflect on the reality of what Abraham Lincoln accomplished with so little.

Extra time may be warranted, but it is always good to see whether the real problem is a lack of structure and compelling language.

The *I Have a Dream* speech does not provide much contrast to Lincoln's masterpiece in terms of delivery time. Martin Luther King delivered his pivotal words in about 17 minutes. Although five times longer than the Gettysburg Address, 17 minutes is still brief by most public speaking standards.

Political speeches and state of the union addresses are often two or three times longer than *I have a Dream* which arguably altered the political landscape during King's lifetime.

Another, more contemporary example of the power of brevity, would be the speech that many agree transformed Barrack Obama from an unknown Senator into a future president. When he addressed the crowd at the 2004 Democratic National Committee he walked onto the stage as an unknown, but less than 20 minutes later, everything changed.

You want to make an impact on your audience and it is worth considering the examples provided by history which demonstrate the fact that impact and brevity often go hand in hand.

CLINCHING THE FINALE

"And...Ok, that looks like the last slide. That's pretty much all I have. Any questions? No? Okay, thank you."

Plenty of presentations end in similar fashion to the preceding statement. It is acceptable, but it also feels like everything just ran out of gas and rolled to the side. The quality of the content and the value of the briefing should not be diminished as a result, but it is a lost opportunity.

People like "bookends." That is to say, presentations that end with similar tone and style as they begin. Maybe you prefer to think of it as a sandwich; one slice of bread on top and one slice of bread on bottom.

Many stories and movies begin and end with the mirror image events, dialogues, settings, and characters. Perhaps a man and wife are driving down a road on a sunny day at the start of the story. The final scene puts them in the same situation, only now, everything about their lives and situation is different. Even if they are going to the same destination as the start (a friend's house, for instance) the reason and consequence of the journey may now be completely different.

It is a powerful way to reach back into the short-term memory of the audience and reel in everything from the start into the closing moment. No matter how good everything up to that closing scene was, the effect of reflecting on the situation with a new perspective doubles the impact of the message.

Remember the Anticipatory Set:

In a previous section, there was a suggestion of using a question as a book-end; "Are chaplains an essential part of the leadership team?"

The content of the briefing should be geared toward persuading the audience in the direction of "yes." When the question is repeated at the end, the audience is forced to remember what their thoughts and feelings were in light of what they know now. Suddenly the content in between is brought to life and given a small bit of permanence in the audience's mind.

No matter what your anticipatory set was, you can close by revisiting it. Maybe you gave a small quiz. Give the quiz again and allow them to see what they learned. Maybe there was an opening quote:

> *"You may write me down in history with your bitter, twisted lies.*
> *You may tread me in the very dirt but still, like dust, I rise"*
> *—Maya Angelou*

Maybe your presentation was on the influence of women in western literature and political thought. If so, the preceding quote at the beginning would generate the right kind of anticipation. However, if you show the same quote again as part of your closing and ask, "does this quote have new meaning for anyone?" It will have an impact and leave a good impression of the overall presentation.

Prepare a statement or closing sentiment

It does not need to be genius or worthy of becoming quoted in future presentations. The final statement will not make or break you as a presenter and it will not change the value of the presentation's content. The closing statement can be very simple, predictable, and short. However, there are two advantages to a deliberate closing statement.

1. The presentation will not simply drift off. It will have a succinct ending, much like "the end" on the last page of the story. The reader knows it is the end, but it provides that little bit of definitive closure.

2. It gives you a confident way to complete your brief. You know what you are going to say and how you are going to say it. It will sound planned which also sounds professional. It is the difference between simply crossing the finish line of a 10K Run and actually breaking the finish line tape with your chest as you cross the finish the line.

MAKE SURE IT IS THE RIGHT TIME

When you are out of time, you are out of time. Briefing schedules are often regimented and simply carrying on for an additional ten minutes is not going to happen. That doesn't mean that you don't have some buffer built in and it also doesn't mean you have to use every minute available to you.

As you near the end, simply ask a question like, "can anyone tell me something interesting they learned today?" This will open up a couple of comments but, more importantly, it will help you gauge the degree to which your message connected. If you ask one or two specific questions and get the feeling that the audience missed the main point, you can revisit one or two topics for clarity (just a few minutes).

For the most part, you should have a gut feeling about whether an audience has stayed with you on the journey, or already came to the room knowing more than they needed to.

You determine the best time to close the briefing.

HOW

PART SEVEN: REVISITING STAGE FRIGHT

Overcoming the World's Number One Fear

The topics of stage fright and the fear of public speaking have been sprinkled throughout this book. This small section will serve as a quick reference repository for the tips and tricks mentioned thus far.

> *"There are only two types of speakers in the world.*
> *1. The nervous and 2. Liars."—Mark Twain*

1. **Do not forget that you are not alone.** Musical and athletic talents may be sprinkled sparingly amidst the population, but anxiety prior to a presentation is as common as it gets…even for those well-known performers and athletes.

2. **Most audience members are not particularly interested in judging your performance.** They just want to receive some information or have a discussion. It may feel like you have a bullseye on your head, but you are really just a central source of information.

3. **No one really wants to switch places with you. They empathize with your position.** The standard sentiment of "I could do that person's job easy, I could take it over anytime they needed me too." rarely applies to public speaking and presentations. Even if

you conduct an average presentation, you provided the audience with a great service. They did not have to be you today. There is a little more grace and appreciation for your task than in most things you do.

4. **Set your expectations to allow some negative comments or input.** There is a tremendous difference between keeping your fingers crossed that no one will heckle, harass, or ask any heated questions, and knowing that it is likely to happen and simply being ready for it. Instead of tensing up and feeling targeted, you just go to business as usual. *Imagine a 2nd Baseman that kept their fingers crossed about a runner trying to steal the base as opposed to training for the certainty of it.*

5. **You have allies.** For every person that is secretly looking to sharp-shoot you, there is someone out there who will have little tolerance for such behavior. Just know that most people have been in the shoes of the presenter and no one likes a bully. The more difficult an audience member gets the more you will generate empathy and support from the rest of the audience.

6. **Bring an accomplice or moral supporter.** Having a co-worker or friend that resides in the audience with the job of helping you keep track of time and your agenda can be very reassuring. It may only be one or two glances, but there is something about knowing you can glance over and get a glimpse of moral support or assistance. Maybe they ask the first question to get the ball rolling. Maybe they are not needed. The benefit is just knowing they are there.

7. **Rehearse and memorize.** Few things provide the natural confidence and defense against stage fright quite like knowing that you know your stuff. Would you rather improvise in public or have your routine ironed out?

8. **Breathing and shoulder tension.** The occasional check on your own shoulder tension is always beneficial. Deliberately relaxing your shoulders sends a subtle signal to the rest of your body that everything is okay. Also, when you have a natural pause where the audience is reading a chart you can also slip in those slow deliberate breaths (in through the nose and out through the mouth). Not in such a way that the audience notices, but find a way to break the cycle of accelerated breathing whenever you can.

9. **Keep your body language and vocal tones subdued.** Nervousness will naturally give you the impulse to pace back and forth, use more hand gestures, and speak in greater tone fluctuations. Keeping a deliberate check on these mannerisms will reflexively keep nervousness in check. Much like taking a deep breath, centering your body movements will center your emotions as well. The briefing may benefit from a more animated speaker, but maintaining self-control and confidence should take precedence.

10. **Revisit friendly faces and avoid direct eye contact.** There will be at least one friendly face in a crowd, and it is helpful to look in their direction from time to time for reassurance. Other than that, you do need to work the room with your eyes. That does not mean that you need to make a lot of eye contact. You can look at people's foreheads, ears, chins, or the space between two people. From ten feet away or more these focal points will have the same effect as eye contact or just the general perception that you are engaging the audience effectively.

11. **Minimize humor.** Humor is a natural go-to mechanism when you are nervous. It is a natural tension breaker and usually connects you to another person in the moment. However, if you are not comfortable as a speaker, have much experience, or simply do not know the audience very well, then humor can be a good way to race to the bottom. Humor relies on timing and appropriate-

ness. Both of those elements are at great risk when you are in new territory or nervous. The bottom line is, you want to minimize risks and avoid coming across as nervous because of nervous humor.

12. **Speak slowly.** This is similar to subdued body language. When you focus on keeping a slow, even rhythm (not monotone or boring, however) then you are keeping your focus where it is most beneficial, on your words and talking points. This allows your attention to stay on content and not start wondering into other distractions such as whether or not someone is judging you. Your nervous energy might simply tune all the way out as soon as you start an even, confident, meticulous string of sentences. If you sound calm and in control, you just might be calm and in control

PART EIGHT: ADVANCED TOPICS

Moving from Professional to Performer

THE POWER OF PERFORMANCE: LESSONS FROM THE WORLD OF STAGE MAGIC

Whether it is a street performer downtown with a table and deck of cards, or a high-profile illusion routine in Las Vegas. Magicians are more than just subtle physical performers who understand deception. They are highly skilled in the art of drawing an audience in, manipulating attention, directing and redirecting expectations and emotions, and proving a stunning pay-off.

It is part mass hypnosis and part story telling.

It does not happen overnight. Even a magician with the best performance instincts learned how to fall flat on their face many times before they began to hold an audience in the palm of their hand. The longer you spend in front of audiences the more comfortable you will become with the status quo and more willing you will be to seek out new challenges.

Stepping into the realm of audience captivation versus merely keeping their attention is one way to take chances and grow as a presenter.

No, this does not mean buying props or strange clothing, hiring assistants, or learning dramatic hand and body movements. The subtlest performers have much in common with the ones that rely on flash-bang special effects and strobe lights.

In fact, there more subtle ones are often the most stunning. In the following example of stage magic brought into the realm of boring annual security briefs, we will introduce Mr. Smith from the Division Cyber Security Office.

1. Mr. Smith introduces himself and starts with an ice-breaker. **This initial comment or demonstration is both humorous and simultaneously demonstrates who he is and why he is there.**

    "Hello everyone. I'm Mr. Smith from the Division Cyber Security office, and I am here to speak to you today about cyber security and system vulnerabilities." (While speaking he is ignoring the crowd and typing into a laptop that is on a podium)

    "Of course," he continues, "I just would appreciate it if everyone would check their cell phones and make sure they are on vibrate." (Continues to type and ignore crowd. "Are we good? Alright." (Turns attention to crowd while looking at an officer in front) "Sorry sir," (He gestures to ranking individual in audience) "I know I was distracted and you are the sort of person who needs to answer all your calls, but I really do need you to turn your ringer down."

    "What? Me?" the identified individual states with little patience. "I'm tracking. Get rolling."

"Okay," Mr. Smith says while pressing one key on the laptop. As soon as he presses the key the identified individual's phone rings loudly. "Well, sir, your phone was turned down but it was not secure. Now, that phone and all its contents are technically mine. Sorry about that."

Of course, it becomes clear that it was a staged introduction for effect, but only after the participant plays it out for another few seconds.

2. **Turn the introduction in a few talking points that lay the ground work for an expected outcome later during the show.** In this case, the expected outcome is that the presenter will use another person in the audience to pull another fake-out.

"Now, who here thinks that, as an enemy cyber agent, I could not actually do that to one of your cell phones? (short discussion follows)

What else do you think I could do that involved your phones? (more discussion)

What do I need in terms of equipment to pull that sort of thing off and how close to you do I need to get in a public place to compromise your devices? (As the discussion continues people start to look nervous and uncomfortable because they realize how vulnerable they are.)

Note, that thus far the presenter has not had to use any slides and has mostly presented several questions for audience participation. Meanwhile, he is making a point that is sinking in on an emotional level.

"Now," Mr. Smith continues, "It was pretty obvious that me and the Major up here were in on that introduction. So, like most magicians, I just put a plant in the audience. Right? Hey, has anyone started to wonder if there are other plants out there? How many people have I staged in the crowd and what might they be up to?"

(Everyone looks around in a combination of curiosity, wonder, and mild paranoia. The emotional response to the topic is starting to work more intensely.) In such a way, Mr. Smith would be meeting his intent of increase awareness without so much a single fact, figure, chart, or true story ripped from today's headlines.

"Wait," Mr. Smith says, "look at you, are all trying to tell me that you all suddenly distrust your co-workers? Hmmmm. Maybe that is all I wanted all along. Maybe that was my actual evil plan. My work here is done." (audience shifts emotionally to varied responses and looks of surprise.)

The audience was expecting another fake-out, but instead received a second lesson about letting your guard down in the workplace and the reality of internal threats. This portion also required no PowerPoint slides, no statistics, no real-world scenarios, and registered on an emotional level in almost no time at all.

The presentation is barely five minutes old and it is already a memorable one that could realistically improve cyber security in the workplace.

3.   After covering some statistics, charts, and stories, Mr. Smith will present the finale. **It will be another trick, but not one that the audience is expecting based on the false expectations that have been established.** Hence, even though the trick itself may not be that impressive, it is not what anyone was looking for.

"I can tell by looking around that you have been in extra-vigilant-mode during this presentation. I am sort of proud of the fact that I almost trained you to be on the lookout for more sneaky tricks... Yes, Sergeant, I'm looking at you. You should see how you guys have been keeping an eye on me and your buddies out of the corner of your eye. This is great stuff. I don't know, I do have one more trick up my sleeve and it does involve another accomplice out there. I don't know though, you are all pretty vigilant now."

The last sentence creates the anticipation of one more big trick and sets expectations that someone amongst them is working with the presenter.

"Now, I just want to introduce you to something we have been seeing out there as a newer threat. Remember when we talked about the types of devices that could read your credit cards and get into your cell phones from a short distance away? Well, now they have made them even smaller. We recently caught someone with this device and they were using it to steal co-workers credit card data right out of their wallets without even touching them."

On the screen Mr. Smith shows an enlarged photo of a tie-clip with a raised crest on it and explains that the crest portion was actually a concealed scanner. At that point, someone raises their hands and says, "Oh, ha-ha, Mr. Smith. I gotcha. You mean like the exact tie clip on your partner at the door with the clip board who checked out I.D. Cards? Very funny."

Mr. Smith looks confused, "Uhm, what? I don't have an assistant and you don't need an I.D. card to attend this brief. Are all of your cards compromised? How did you even know that person was here in an official capacity?"

The audience is wowed by the out-of-the-box final trick but they are not entirely sure they know what is going on. They were not looking for that angle. Then, another gentleman walks onto the stage and introduces himself as Mr. Smith and apologizes for being late.

The audience is now completely mystified as Mr. Smith number one turns to them and says, "What? just because I told all of you I was 'Mr. Smith from Division Cyber Security' you just let me keep all of you here as a captive audience? Does your division even have a Cyber Security section? What if all this was just to distract you and your new heightened levels of vigilance from my real plan?" He yells while pointing his finger in the air.

The lights go out.

Mr. Smith, "An attack on your power grid!"

Lights pop on.

Mr. Smith, "Thank you everyone! I hope this was an effective presentation and I trust you will never look at your world the same again!"

Very subtle, very much a great performance, and very effective at driving the content home on an emotional level. Also, when it comes to making a point with very few slides, talking points, or memorized material, it is almost easier. It simply takes a great deal of confidence, some acting ability, and a great sense of timing.

THE POWER OF STORY

The power of story is closely related and integrated into the art of performance.

There are a couple of different ways to look at integrating the power of story into your presentation. The first is the most straight forward method. Just to add a story as part of your introduction or as a way to add emphasis throughout the presentation.

If you are conducting a long presentation over the course of two or more hours, then integrating a story into the top of each hour or as part of a return from breaks is a good way to help decompress and avoid information overload.

It might not be hard to find a story that works with your presentation. Stories, at their heart, are merely ways in which people communicate personal experiences and problems. Maybe you have a personal connection to the topic at hand.

"Before we get started I wanted to share with you a quick story about why this topic is meaningful to me. Just about the time I joined the Army someone told me that..."

Maybe you are already curious how that sentence ended and what the story may be. That is just how effective storytelling is. Our brains seem to be wired to either absorb the world through story or communicate to others in the same way. How many conversations at work start with something along the lines of:

"So, I stop by the Headquarters building, right? And I noticed that there is just no parking spaces at all. And I'm thinking, this is weird for a Thursday morning. Did I miss something?.."

or

"Well, the weekend was pretty boring, although going to the mall was a little more exciting than normal. I have to take a detour because of the construction, but I must have spaced out and missed a turn, because I ended up over by..."

ART OF PERSUASION
It is difficult to completely avoid using at least a few story elements in any presentation simply because of how natural the approach is. Even the format of a presentation is beginning—middle—the end. But you can look at some elements of story and use them to enhance the substance of your presentation. Once you become aware of it, you may find that some of the most persuasive speakers and effective politicians understand this approach.

First, a couple of basic techniques that both novelists and screenwriters use to keep readers turning pages and audiences glued to their seats. Yes, you need larger themes, a good premise, plot, subplots, etc. But that is not enough to keep scenes from falling flat. There are countless, deliberately crafted micro-moments that fill the pages of your favorite books and screenplays.

Good News/Bad News:

Two unwatchable stories would be:

1) good things keep happening to the main character as they go about their day and then they solve a problem, the end.

2) The main character experiences set-back after set-back, no turn arounds, no bright spots, no sudden revelation about how to solve the problem then, everything just fizzles out, the end.

You would probably walk out half-way through in each case. So, here is how it works, it's not really a matter of creating ups and downs throughout some story curve so much as it is about creating ups and downs from moment to moment. This is the good news/bad news technique.

"Oh, wow, this card has a check for $10,000 inside!" and then the guy who said that gets immediately slapped in the face by his sister.

"Hey, good news! That phone call you've been waiting for is on line one." Character picks up phone looking excited with fingers crossed and then the excited facial expression turns to gloom as the muffled words come through the line.

This is how story lines "breath."

You want your presentation to breath, so you can borrow this concept.

"As you can see here, violent crimes are trending downward. Same on this chart with regard to murder, and here you can see aggravated assault also on the decline. However, now you can see that in the last year, unfortunately, sexual assaults are on the rise."

"Last year we had our third straight year of declines in overall breaches to our cyber security. But in that same period of time the number attempts increased exponentially and are becoming very sophisticated."

Your presentation probably already has elements of good news and bad news in them. You merely need to go into editing mode and weave them in such a way that the good news/bad news aspect accordion back and forth.

Question/Answer:

After reading the previous section you probably get the idea. A story usually works toward resolving one or two major questions such as, "Will the hero manage to rescue his brother from the outlaw gang?" or "Is the hero's mother actually the serial killer?"

Those are the sorts of questions that can keep people paying attention until the end. Can you identify a primary question that your briefing answers?

"Is there a correlation between population growth and violence?"

"Is the chaplain an integral part of the leadership team?"

"Are we ready for the next challenges in cyber security?"

If the question is already there if you are burying it in a topic header i.e. "Our Current Cyber Security Posture," then you probably want to make that change. You may not have a choice because some formats are rigidly fixed, but if you have the option to turn a topic header into a question, then do it.

However, just as the good news/bad news technique, you need micro momentum. The more slides you can introduce with a question and finish with an answer the better. Ask a question on slide two, but delay the answer until slide seven. Mix and match short range questions with medium and long-range questions? People just can't help but wanting to know the answer to a question, even if the topic is only mildly interesting.

Ticking Clock(s):

A scene shows two men at a table in a restaurant having a discussion about a tense situation at work. Okay, that might be interesting depending on the topic. And then camera pans down to beneath the table top and we see that a bomb is taped underneath with two minutes left on the counter. Game changer. Now, you have a "ticking clock" in your scene and every single move that everyone in that restaurant makes for the next two minutes will be of consequence.

There are all kinds of ways to insert a ticking clock. It can be a deadline for a project or homework assignment. Maybe everyone is waiting for a character to return, or even for a change of season. Another example has something to do with money that must be paid to someone by a certain time. Etc. Then again, bombs work really well and plenty of movies use them.

You, on the other hand, do not want to even talk about them, unless of course, you are briefing about ordinance or ordinance disposal.

It is a little-known fact that the famous Death Star run in the first Star Wars movie did not include the "ticking clock" of the rebel planet's pending incineration. It was added at the last minute during editing by combining outtakes from different sequences. Some have argued that without this single change the franchise may have never taken off.

So, how do you get a ticking clock into your presentation?

Literally: "Okay, I've learned that if I don't cover this slide in less than five minutes I start to run into issues later on. Can someone keep time for me? Thanks!" and then ask for an update every 45 seconds or so. Of course, you will know full well that it is not really an issue, but that is not the point. It is just another opportunity to get eyes glued to the screen.

"Okay, so, once again we will see how each side of the room does. Here are the questions and there is one minute to decide, as a group, what you choose as the answers. Ready? Start."

"If you can bear with me for literally seven more minutes, then we will be ready to break for lunch. Someone keep me honest, now. Don't let me go over. You got it over there? Okay, she is the official time. Let's finish."

If you can find a way to punctuate your presentation with a few ticking clock moments it will breath more life into your presentation.

A Villain:

Yes, you need a villain. What is a hero without a good villain? If superheroes just fought rank and file criminals every day, then no one would care. Sounds too dramatic? Your presentation about the number of training days before the next field problem doesn't require a villain?

In fact, there is already a built-in villain, you just need to tweak the way you talk about it such that people start to develop a natural sense of wanting to defeat it. If that vibe shows up at all, then you can consider the energy level of the room to be raised. Here are some examples.

Cyber Security	→	Cyber Threats, Insider Threats, Poor Protocols
SHARP	→	Ignorance, Apathy
Crime	→	Problematic education system, Police department in need of modernization
Lower PT Scores	→	Lack of Leader involvement

When all else fails, you can always default to the all-purpose villain of time itself. When are you and your peers not working against time? There is always a countdown to an event, a budget deadline, a field problem, a ceremony, awards and evaluations deadlines, etc. and never enough time.

Getting a lot done in a short amount of time will require team work and an awareness that everyone is in the same boat. You will have to mention time repeatedly in several briefs. Why not make sure you add a few more references and say the same thing in different ways to make it interesting.

ADV. TOPICS

Slide One: "...As you can see, we are still on trajectory, but one week will go quickly."

Slide Two: "...And here is that three-day weekend, so we need to keep that in mind..."

Slide Three: "...When we meet again to finalize this milestone we will only have two days left to complete the entire thing..."

Slide Four: "...I am pretty sure that one day is enough for that, if not, there is not much room for error."

It would be hard to not feel the weight of the clock after that briefing. It is a common enemy and everyone needs to help.

It is not complicated, nor does it take much creativity. You merely have to define a villain based on the nature of your presentation and make a point to reference that villain throughout. Connect the villain to the solution and a team effort. It is a passive, but natural way to energize a presentation and increases persuasion.

PART NINE: LISTS

Quick Reference for Success

REACH THE AUDIENCE BY SPEAKING THEIR LANGUAGE

You are not trying to instruct or persuade yourself, it's about the them.

- Show you care by doing your research—

  - What the audience value?

  - Who are their leaders and how they rose through the ranks?

  - What are their organizational philosophies and vision statements?

  - What are their goals and recent achievements?

  - What are the proprietary phrases and buzz words

  - Do they have any ongoing campaigns?

  - Give them a chance to talk about themselves

- Understand their challenges and resources

- Get involved before-hand and communicate with any pertinent experts in their ranks.

- Watch out for Acronyms
- What major events do they have in the near term?
- Be ready to address questions and concerns from personality types that are very different from you
- Be ready to present your most important topics from different angles
- What is the human aspect of your topic?
- How does this impact people?
- What are the second and third order effects on the organization?
- **How can you help them win?**

Your ideas are great, but why should they care?

- Provide plain, clear, and concise information that they can utilize for their purposes.
- Do not talk down or patronize
- Be Flexible
- Keep and cool without taking resistance personal
- **What is the single thing that defines success for this group?**

CLASSROOM MANAGEMENT

Stay cool, calm, collected and in charge of the briefing

You are in charge, and you decide how to adjust fire during the engagement.

- Use redirecting cues: Just rehearse a couple and be ready to use them

    "And that…is precisely the direction I would like to see this discussion go, and the last couple of slides cover that question…"

    "Excellent comment, that is something we get into during/when…"

"Interesting. I think we'll be able to explore that near the end, but the next couple of charts will help clarify."

- Don't confuse the idea controlling a room during a presentation with "being the boss"...unless, of course; you are the boss.

- Try the "lowered boom" technique

- Start your presentation with a smile

- Wait for the first side-bar conversation or whispering voice in the audience

- Lower the boom by calmly and assertively addressing the sidebar and asking for their attention

- Don't allow questions or comments to go from zero to personal

- Most moments are zero percent personal and at least 80% opportunity

- **Respond to all interactions from the high ground with respect and humility**

- *Win the energy in a room and strangers to your side.*

- Emotionally flat on the outside says, 'cool and confident on the inside

  - Deal with hecklers by verbally, not emotionally, responding

  - Show you have a sense of humor, but that you are there for business.

- When a bully does strike, then know that time, and the room, are on your side.

- You can go out on a limb and be professionally assertive with a bully.

- People generally see self-defense as a right.

- However, make sure you have read the yourself and the room correctly.

BE YOURSELF

Conducting a brief can throw stress and unpleasant surprises your way. Meeting every challenge in a way that is most natural to you ensure the fewest missteps.

1. Do not try to "sound smart." No matter what the topic or the audience, when you do not use language that is natural to you, it will show.

2. Avoid jargon and big words

3. People want sincerity and basic competence

4. The only worse than insincerity is pretentiousness

5. Relax, read the room and follow your instincts about the audience

6. Be flexible. You are there to accomplish an intent, not an exact plan

7. Respect your natural tendencies regarding body language, humor, etc. and analyze what is best for the environment and audience

8. Being yourself means knowing your strengths and weaknesses

9. Seek a co-worker for advice and rehearse to make sure you put your best qualities on display.

PERSONALITY TYPES

Some of the folks you may meet during your briefing

· *Worst Case Personality*

This is the last person that would want to brief. Think of someone that meets that definition and have a plan if someone similar shows up.

○ Be ready for the worst and everything after that is relatively easy.

- Consider creating a "hidden-slide" or separate page of references
- Expect to shift on a moment's notice

- ***The Hard Charger***

Successful people in the both the military and business often have a hard charger personality type. Will have no qualms about interrupting you at any time, with any critique; even when you are mid-sentence. Hard chargers want to move the organization down the field and take the goal post

- Embrace the interruption and provide a concise answer.
- Cue a slide from later in the deck to facilitate your answer. Show you are ready and unintimidated.
- They want to know you are knowledgeable and prepared
- Expect them to back off after you show you can handle yourself.
- Does your presentation focus on the winning?
- If nothing else, keep that 'this is a win' mentality in your tone and body language.

- ***The Rabbit Trailer***

Creative Types who are pleasant, crack jokes and find new ideas and think your information genuinely fascinating. They also can't help but daydream and start asking "but what if..." questions.

- Just expect it.
- It is not an insult, or an inconvenience as much as it is just part of the game.
- If you take it personally or seem flustered by the diversion, it will show. This could shift the tone of the room away from embracing you your briefing.
- Try to redirect comments as pertinent during the next few slides
- State that those are fascinating questions to address at the end

- ○ Run with them for a little bit but don't let the diversion spiral out of control

- ○ *Think of such moments as an opportunity to enhance anticipation for the rest of the brief as opposed to a detractor.*

- ### The Empath

Individual who seems hardwired for compassion and empathy. Will tend to support you in any way they can if you seem to be stumbling, losing the crowd, or otherwise need some assistance. That's great, but

a. You aren't there to be supported or assisted. You are there to assist, inform, and in some way, support the group's mission.

b. Appreciate this perspective and work it into your presentation when you hear it.

c. *If you are a logic driven personalities you could use their insight.*

- ### The Networker

Networkers look for new doors, alliances, solutions through human resources. They do not see organizational success as something that can be attained in a vacuum or on an island.

- ○ *Does your presentation address how the talking points address other organizations connected to the audience?*

- ○ *Can you demonstrate how your proposal contributes to networking*

- ○ *Does your presentation look at the big picture and suggest networking opportunities?*

AUDIENCE TYPES

The Most Common Groups You Will Address

Audience 1: Your Own Organization

It is usually a good thing to play on your turf.

Advantages:

- You can conduct rehearsals at your leisure.

- You don't have to worry that you left something "back at the office"

- You won't lose any time or assume any risk getting from Point A to Point B.

- You know who is who; the formal and informal power structure.

- You know the personality types

- You know what drives the decision-making process

- You understand the ins and outs of talking to the decision makers.

Disadvantages:

- Baggage or grudges between you and anyone else will enter the briefing room with you.

- No one in the audience has any illusions about who you are, what you know, and your general level of experience.

- Possible subtext and static between you and your message

- Don't be too comfortable or casual

You can relax with the home team, but you cannot take anything for granted.

Audience 2: Unfamiliar Territory

When you conduct a briefing in an unfamiliar setting to an audience of strangers you are at the ultimate audience disadvantage. Look at the advantages first.

Advantages:

- No pre-existing baggage or friction with anyone on the team
- The tendency to be viewed as a guest and start with some slack.
- The organization will want to show its best side and courtesy
- A great opportunity to represent your organization and broaden your personal reputation

Disadvantages:

- You will know nothing about the command climate, leadership styles, communication styles, etc.
- Don't understand who does what or what the levels of subject matter expertise are.
- You will be unfamiliar with organizational standards, habits, and expectations.

Keeping calm and remaining flexible is the name of the game. The less you rely on each step of your briefing 'going according to plan,' the less stress you will have when you experience negativity, distractions, misunderstandings, and friction..

Audience 3: The Uniform (Homogenous) Crowd

In general, the uniform or homogenous crowd is less challenging. As a Soldier, you could throw around a few acronyms and regulatory references without losing a single member of the audience. In fact, you could probably talk shop all day and get away with it. You could even tell inside jokes with people you don't even know.

Advantage:

- The uniform crowd makes life easy if you know the ropes.
- Disadvantages:
- This group will unilaterally know when you get it wrong.
- They will not extend you much grace if you are one of them.

Audience 4: The Variable Crowd

The less homogenous your audience is, the more likely it is that any given point of your presentation will strike a wrong chord with someone. While it probably isn't your mission to make all the people happy all the time it is your mission to keep disruptions and emotions to a minimum

How to prepare:

- Use some latitude and contemplate the audience you are about to face. Look at the topics that come up and consider the implications from every walk of life.
- Don't auto-pilot and fail to review your material for changes, there should be few issues.
- What is it that you want the audience to take away and what is the simplest path there?
- You may be surprised how much you can cut from a questionable presentation and how much common ground you can find for all participants.

Despite surface appearances, most people share similar goals and values.

Audience 5: The Big Cheese

A small group led by a commander or ranking individual. What the boss thinks is all that matters. Regardless of the other participants, you should remember that you are always speaking directly to the boss, and more specifically, to the boss's priorities and concerns. Other people in the room may throw out hard questions and even seem critical They are applying their knowledge and experience for the boss's benefit.

Recommendations:

- No "tap-dancing."
- Expect interruptions and tough questions
- Deflate stress by politely asking for clarification if needed.
- Don't show the audience you are embarrassed.
- If you do not know something, simply be honest about it. Let them know that will get the answer immediately afterward.

Audience 6: The Panel

Think an X-Factor or American Idol audition

Advantage:

- You have a greater chance of finding at least one ally or someone who understands your point of view. Even one ally can help start to sway the panel

Disadvantages:

- It is difficult to meet the expectations of one person but more difficult to do so with three or more people who share equal influence.
- You will likely face rounds of questions from multiple directions.
- It may feel more like an interrogation than ordinary Q and A
- You may have the issue of more than one panel member that is overtly unreceptive or difficult.

Know your stuff AND be quick to admit when you don't. See who emerge as an ally or advocate. The more you rehearse, the less strange the panel situation is. Remember, if it feels like an interrogation, simply give yourself a few seconds to compose your answer in your head before you start talking. You have some control over the momentum in the room.

HECKLERS, SHARPSHOOTERS, AND ASSASSINS

The Less Pleasant Audience Members

- Expecting them is half the battle.
- Why get rattled or take it personal when you know it's coming and you are ready for it.
- Shoot for emotional flatness
- Emotionally flat on the outside says, 'cool and confident on the inside'

HECKLERS

This is often just the office joker doing their thing. Laugh a little at yourself and reply with an even comeback.

- Handling them without encouraging them.
- Don't be a willing accomplice they are likely to keep rolling until the boss shuts them down.
- Verbally but not emotionally embrace them
- Don't feed into the heckler's actions.
- You have a sense of humor, but that you are there for business.
- If you have little tolerance for clowning or joking in the workplace you will be tempted to reprimand or slam the door on the heckler. This section will address such a tactic, but using it on the heckler will usually come across as a negative.

SHARPSHOOTERS

These interrupters bring some degree of malice.

- Be proactive by eliminating grammatical errors, factual errors, outdated references, etc.

- If they mean you ill, then nothing defeats them quite like being visibly cool.

- If you deserve it, then taking your medicine with a no-excuses

- If the sharpshooter is ranking individual, then accept it as mentorship and maybe even write down a quick note on the spot. People in such a position often require that others take literal notes when an issue is called out.

ASSASSINS

This could be an individual who either doesn't like you, or is militantly against whatever it is you are selling to the audience. Maybe they are just "shooting the messenger" which happens to be you. Maybe they want derail you entirely and/or destroy your message. It could actually be personal, and it will always feel personal.

- Remember emotional flatness.

- The good news is, no one likes an assassin.

- Time, and the room, are on your side.

- Uou can go out on a limb and be professionally assertive with an assassin.

INFORMATIVE AND PERSUASIVE PRESENTATIONS

Some Suggestions for Success

Persuasive

The persuasive environment is one in which you are working against the odds. Your goal is to change their minds and bring them to your side. A sales presentation will often fall into this category. You might call it an adversarial process since you are starting off at odds with the audience. Here is a formula that is detailed in the "What" section of the book.

- **Present your intentions in neutral, positive, or harmless terms.**

- **Demonstrate knowledge, respect, and empathy with their values or goals**

- **Turn the negative message into a positive**
  Your contrary idea is probably misunderstood. Reframe it, put in their context.

- **Antony invokes the crowd's previous feelings and beliefs**
  Find where they once had a similar approach or value and demonstrate its validity

- **Openly advocate for your position, but now the meaning is redefined in their view point**

The art of persuasion is fundamental to several professions and useful to everyone at some point in their life. keep the fundamentals in mind.

- Research your audience

- Actively listen to participants

- Courtesy and respect always

- Keep Cool

- Anticipate objections and critiques

- Know your subject in depth

- Set your expectations appropriately

The Informative Presentation

This is the more common type of presentation. The audience is there of some mutual concern and will start gathering, consolidating, discussing, and deciding on information. An adversarial process isn't necessary. Since the productivity of the group is the goal, consider these pointers.

- Streamline for maximum effectiveness.

- But, do not cut content down to the point where you simply go for the absolute minimum.

- Find those three to five topics or points that are most important or new and then go into as much depth as possible.

- Provide a review of the older information

- Leave some room to cover portions in depth if the need arises.

- Demonstrate that you know what's unimportant

- Simultaneously putting some depth and passion into the main points will convey professionalism and respect for the audiences' time.

QUESTION AND ANSWER VS. LECTURE FORMAT

Some Suggestions for Success

Q and A/Discussion Format

The question and answer format is the preferable format in almost any context, facilitates discussion, which facilitates the audiences' investment in the content limits the amount of information you can cram into your allotted time, requires confidence and skill in front of an audience

- Can be more difficult to manage the time available

- Often difficult to keep on track
- Have your head in the right place as you plan your questions and rehearse possible responses to the answers.
- Become familiar with the Socratic Method (detailed in "What" section of book.
- Socratic Method is time consuming so set expectations appropriately.
- Don't ask questions just to ask questions. Consider that some of your questions may be pointless or obvious and delete them.

Lecture Format—Seek Clarity

The briefing that consists almost entirely of a lecture format is direct, inherently authoritative, and time conscious, using this time efficiently as opposed to abusing it.

- Active voice set within well-organized short sentences will always shine.
- Does not have to be boring.
- Decide the main point and three supporting points you want your briefing to communicate.
- Look at each slide or chart and identify the single thing the audience should learn from it. From that skeleton, you should be able to build an effective, compelling lecture.

PRESENTING A HIGHLY TECHNICAL TOPIC

Some Suggestions for Success

Technical Topics

Convey highly technical or detailed information and present a high risk of making the audience "drink from the firehose." You will lose them one by one if you push technical details too hard or too fast

- Perform frequent checks on learning.

- Every segment of a presentation should include an opportunity to engage the audience

- The more technical the presentation, the more frequently you should include checks on learning.

- Q and A session allows people to tag onto an answer or interject questions and comments.

But don't just plan checks on learning, plan to adjust or revisit entire segments as a result.

- Be Flexible.

- Information is exhausting.

- Frequently scan the audience for confused or vacant looks.

- Rehearse. Run your presentation by someone who represents your audience. Make sure you are maintaining an even balance of time and information.

HOW TO OVERCOME THE DISADVANTAGE OF AN AWAY GAME

Some Suggestions for Success

Location Matters

Ask yourself these questions about the location where you will present your briefing.

- What the condition the room will be in when you arrive?

- Who are the points of contact for reserving the room and getting it rearranged?

- How do you switch back and forth between screens and turn on all the equipment?

- What will the room temperature be?

- Where is the thermostat?

- How many chairs are available and where to get extras?

- If you need more copies on site will you be able to use their machine? Do they have one?

- How do you transfer your presentation to their computer?

- Maybe all their computers are restricted from reading CDs and you have to deliver it to the IT manager a week ahead of time.

- Does all their equipment work? Maybe the monitors are out or maybe the PA system is known for being static-ridden and breaking sound up?

- Are you used to moving around when you brief? Is there room for that at the new venue?

- Are you used to a podium? Will they have one there?

- If you inspect the room for proper setup a day ahead of time how do you know it will stay that way? Who oversees that sort of thing?

- What events are taking place at that location prior to your presentation?

- Is there another even immediately after yours? What about immediately before?

- You don't think about the laser pointer, because it is always under the podium or in your desk drawer?

- Which remote does what and which light switches control which light panels?

- Who do you call or grab to fix almost any emergency or shortcoming?

- How long does it take to drive to the location?

- Where will you park?

SYSTEMS CHECKS

How to beat "the gremlins"

- Screens

    - One or two? Do you want the same thing on each or two different but coordinated images?

    - Do they both work? How do you get your product on to the computer or other device that controls them?

    - Do you normally brief with the screen in front of you or to your side? What happens when it is above your head and or behind you?

    - Will you need extra practice to adjust your briefing style to the placement of the graphics?

- Lights

    - Everyone likes extra sets of bright lights in their face when they are engaged in public speaking (just kidding of course). Are you ready for that? Do you plan to rehearse with all the lights on?

    - Is there a major difference in room temperature between the stage and the rest of the room?

    - Do you see yourself needing more water than usual nearby to prevent a dry throat? Maybe you normally don't think about water but now you should.

    - Will the actual presentation involve a darkened auditorium? If so, how well will you be able to see the audience's reactions and level of interest?

- Microphones and PA Systems

    - When was the last time you presented with a microphone?

    - Do you know the right distance to keep it from your mouth?

- Do you have extra batteries for a clip-on microphone?

- How about back-up microphones?

- What causes feedback?

- What resolves feedback?

- If your microphone ultimately fails how loud do you really have to be to compensate?

- Who will run the sound system and assist with any audio-visual issues?

- Will that person be at your rehearsal?

- Do you have any voice inflections, or habits such as over enun-ciating or under enunciating that will play terribly through a PA.

Check any and all systems, microphones, speakers, lights, monitors, projectors, remotes, and laser pointers the day before a presentation. Most major problems can be fixed or adapted to on 24 hours' notice. However, today is always a new day. Everything that you checked yesterday and then put under lock and key until today has the potential to surprise. Don't forget to check one or two hours ahead of the event and then again about 20 minutes out.

CLIMATE ISSUES

- Move the presentation to an earlier time of day: Usually not pos-sible but sometimes it is more than welcome and people will jump at the opportunity (Fridays, for example).

- Request permission to use authorized uniform modifications during the presentation. Simultaneously, if individuals will be in civilian attire then advise participants as soon as possible that more temperate attire is encouraged. This allows them to prepare ahead of time.

- See if you can present the material at a larger venue within your organization. A larger room mitigates the tendency for an audience to heat up the space.

- Open doors and windows well ahead of the presentation and keep them open during the presentation (if security permits). You want an optimum and even temperature at the start of the presentation with as much "fresh air" as possible. Later, when the conference room picks up one to five degrees above the temperature of the other rooms it will create a natural draft and air will flow in and out of the room.

- Remember, a lack of centralized air flow from the ventilation system will also create a concentration of carbon dioxide in enclosed spaces. While not deadly, per se, CO_2 does invite the "sleep monster."

- Fans! Fans are the most common solution and usually available. Most facilities even have a few of giant variety that resemble stage wind machines. But how to employ them. Most people want the fan blowing right on them, but collectively, you are better served if they are at the doors or windows to multiply any natural draft. If you have two entrances try the push-pull method of one fan blowing fresh air in at one door and a second fan pulling warm air out through the other door. You can't fool natural processes, but you can enhance them.

- How loud are the fans? How distracting will the additional sound be? What can you do to mitigate?

- If possible and permissible, have ice cold water, juice, or soda available. You don't necessarily want to encourage an abundance of latrine breaks but holding a cold can or bottle usually makes people feel cooler even if they don't drink the contents.

GENERAL ITEMS TO CHECK AND RECHECK

Some Suggestions for Success

NOTE: Many things can be arranged ahead of time and anything to prevent you from carrying a foot locker of material into the facility on the day of event is preferable, however, verify, verify, verify. Put your eyes or hands on materials on site as close to the event as possible and have a back-up plan.

- ✓ Erasable Markers / Permanent Markers
- ✓ Laser Pointer / Wooden Pointer
- ✓ Podium
- ✓ Butcher Block paper / Stand
- ✓ Number of hard copies needed plus ____ extra
- ✓ Presentation forwarded digitally to POC plus extra copy on CD/DVD
- ✓ Required number of tables and chairs are available and arranged
- ✓ Extra Shirt/Top/Pants in case of last minute spill or stains
- ✓ Monitors Screens work and tested
- ✓ Microphone available and ready
- ✓ PA system set to correct volume and dynamics
- ✓ Lights and changes in lighting are understood/rehearsed
- ✓ POCs are tracking the time, requirements, and will be available for last minute issues
- ✓ Personal Business Cards
- ✓ Parking arranged
- ✓ Average travel time at pertinent time of day is rehearsed
- ✓ Other

Expect the unexpected.

It's not personal, just another day and another opportunity to show your peers that you are bigger than whatever speed bumps land in your path.

PREPARATION CHECKLIST

Victory and Defeat are Usually Determined Before the Battle Begins

- ✓ Prepare Slideshow

- ✓ Update Resource Slides after checking publication dates and sources

- ✓ Rehearse Entire Presentation

- ✓ Memorize key points and definitions

- ✓ Rehearse in front of a peer or target audience member

- ✓ Contact POC to reserve space or confirm time

- ✓ Contact POC to arrange or confirm set-up requirements

- ✓ Check briefing area for equipment functionality and supplies on hand

- ✓ Research latest information on topic

- ✓ Revise notes

- ✓ Print Copies

- ✓ Coordinate POCs to assist with lights/audio/setup/environmental control

- ✓ Reserve enablers (VTC bandwidth, teleconference line reservations, audio/visual, podiums, etc.)

- ✓ Print off large display items (usually requested through installation activity or purchased via commercial source)

- ✓ Arrange coffee, drinks, or snacks

EFFECTIVE REHEARSALS

Some Suggestions for Success

First and Foremost: Rehearse

The more you rehearse your content and develop those exact phrases that you are most comfortable and confident in, the less your brain will have to work during a presentation. Muscle memory is preferable to living in problem solving mode in front of an audience.

Therefore, train as you fight.

- Invite Feedback: Start with a close co-worker and they will likely provide suggestions without any blunt or sharp edges. After this, bring in a supervisor or less "friendly" co-worker. You can expect additional suggestions and a few uncomfortable moments. At some point, you should implement an opportunity for some of all of your audience to provide written, anonymous feedback. That can be very interesting and ultimately taken with a grain of salt. However, you are likely to learn things in this format that you cannot learn by any other method. It's not just about fixing your shortcomings. You also want to maximize your message.

- How long does it *really* take to complete your presentation if you presented it to nothing but an empty room without distraction, how long would it take? If you don't know the answer to that, then you will stumble during your event.

  - When you rehearse, start a stop watch first. Try to simulate realistic pauses and space for the occasional question or sharpshooter.
  - Did you feel crunched?
  - Were you stretching topics out to buy time?
  - Did you run out of questions before you ran out of time?
  - Was your pacing even or did you spend too long on the introduction?
  - Which parts need to be expanded based on audience reactions?
  - Which parts need to shrink or be deleted?

Prepare to Speak but Prepare to Listen:

When you rehearse in front of a co-worker or small test audience ask them to throw at least one wrench into the works every so often. You have to know how your rhythm and emotions fair under realistic conditions. You also need a feel for how much time you may want to allocate for buffer during certain portions of the presentation.

CONDUCTING THE BRIEFING

Some Suggestions for Success

Just as you are preparing to take center stage:

1. Take a moment to center yourself and ensure that you start out relaxed and emotional subdued.

2. Check your shoulder tension. Deliberately decide to relax and drop your shoulders and see what happens

3. Take two or three slow, full breaths in through the nose and out through the mouth. If you are nervous at all, then your breathing is going to be faster and shallower than normal.

✓ Introduce yourself make sure that the audience know who you are and why you are there.

"Hello, I'm SGT Smith and I've spent three years working in the Judge Advocate's office where I frequently assist with cases related to sexual assault. Today's presentation compares incidents of sexual assault in the military to the civilian sector as well as prosecution rates. It sounds like apples to apples comparison at first, but the details are more complicated. Next slide, please."

✓ **Start Looking for the "Lightbulb" Right Away.**

- It is fairly obvious when you strike a chord with someone. Anytime you see it, if you have time, stop and acknowledge their response.

- Look for nods, clock/watch glances, knitted brows, crossed arms, and tilted heads are all sure signs that something is happening out there. If the signals don't match your content or your expectation, then it is time to find out what is going on.

- You don't want to be a mile down the road before you find out you're not just on the wrong track but alienating the audience.

- Demonstrate that you are paying attention by responding to your environment appropriately

✓ Be Ready to Shift Gears flexible

- The nature of your presentation or the timeframe may dictate that you simply plough through any questions or distractions, but practice responding and redirecting in a courteous manner.

- One of the great payouts to research and knowing your topic is gaining almost infinite flexibility.

✓ Humor Working? Great, Don't Push It.

- If you can't help but add a little humor or the situation warrants it, then do your thing.

- If your jokes fall flat, then take the hint.

- Avoid having such a good time that go off course

✓ Eye Contact vs. Eye Aversion

AVOID

- Eyes fixed on the floor or excessive glances upward

- Eyes buried into index/note cards

- Staying focused on the slides and not looking at the audience

- Staring above the audience or around the audience but not at the audience.

- Always returning to the same one or two audience members when you look out

✓ Suggested Techniques

  ○ Instead of gravitating to those friendly faces in the crowd, simply develop a rhythm.

  ○ When you first look out at the crowd go dead center. Always start in the center.

  ○ You don't even have to look at one person in particular.

  ○ You can look at the space between two people. But the next time you look out move to the either the right or left portions of the room.

  ○ Think variety and duration.

  ○ No matter where you fix your gaze you should shoot for a three to five second window.

  ○ You can think, 'look left, look right, look center.' Or perhaps 'noon, three o'clock, six o'clock,' it really doesn't matter. So long as you accomplish variety and a good 3-5 second duration, you are good to go. Practice this. After a while, you will scan the room without thinking.

APPENDIX: SLIDE DO'S AND DON'TS

The following pages illustrate some strong do's and don'ts to keep in mind when putting together your slides for your briefing.

Theses tips will help you turn busy and distracting slides, into a clean and effective presentation.

Slides Are Not A Book

You have a lot to say so say it all. That's one way to look at it, but it is better to learn how to say a lot by saying as little as possible. Your audience may have time to read all this text while you go about your presentation, but how can they concentrate on anything you have to say when they have read the first chapter of your novella while you talk? Of course, this is a big exaggeration, but just look at this slide. Creating anything close to slamming your audience with something like this is a bad idea. Your charts should be sharp, minimalist, enhance your talking points, as opposed to talk for you, and keep your audience from getting eye fatigue or some other form of stress reaction while trying to participate in your event. There once was a man from Pawtucket. The cow jumped over the moon. That is about how anyone reading this slide would start to feel right about now if they were still able to concentrate at all. A Chart is not a book, it is more like a poem. You are likely familiar with the power of a single line of poetry, a single quote from a movie, or a poignant line from a song can cause you to contemplate the mysteries of life for an hour. That is the sort of thing you are shooting for. Which means the opposite of what you see here. Say a lot, but by finding a powerful image, phrase, or discrete set of simple phrases, bullets, or facts, that provoke the audiences mind. Seriously, by now you could have delivered the Gettysburg address twice. Do you really think you are smarter than Abraham Lincoln. Chances are, if you can't say it in a single sentence, you probably can't say it if you have all day to say it. And judging by this slide, It looks like you think you have all day to get your point across. I wonder if anyone in your audience is still paying attention. Did anyone actually read all this? What kind of person has that sort of patience? What sort of person asks a room for of casual acquaintance and strangers to put up with such a thing. Hopefully, your audience will never have to answer those questions.

Slides Are Poetry

- Keep it simple

- Prove you know your stuff

- Put it all into a few well chosen points

- You can afford some style

- But don't go over the top

- Put it all on the line—or as few lines as possible

So Bullet Points are the Answer

- Not Exactly
- See anything wrong here
- Remember,
- The bullet points help you keep it simple
- So why would you do this?
- What kind of impression does this leave?
- What did you think when you first spotted this chart?
- Is that the impression you want to leave?
- Too much is too much
- How do you know when it's too much?
- Take a look at your product, and be honest
- If it doesn't look right it probably isn't right
- If you must have so much on one slide

- Then perhaps you can have some bullet point disappear as an effect and new bullet points take their place
- But that is hardly different from just making another slide
- Or two
- Or maybe, it is just better to figure out the most important points
- And leave it to them
- If it's not simple it probably isn't artistic or creative either
- Cluttered is cluttered
- Too much is too much
- You're probably repeating yourself anyway
- So just stop

Making it Happen!

Oh The Many Themes and Graphics

- Colors are the spice of life but not presentations

- But all this says is "Adjust you monitor settings"

- You wouldn't create a splashy mess on purpose

- But you might accidentally put one or two too many great ideas in one place

- Keep Themes and Backgrounds simple and non-distracting

Too Much

Does Everything Here Belong Here?

Our Market

Match, Don't Mix

- Don't Forget to sign up for the company picnic!

- Marketing Brings Desserts and Sales Brings Main dishes

- Management has approved half-day on Friday

- Turn in your nominations for Outstanding Team Player before COB

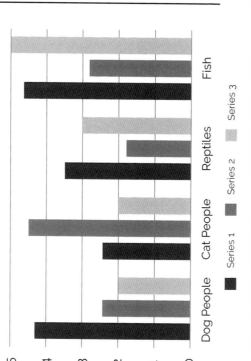

| | Series 1 | Series 2 | Series 3 |

Dog People • Cat People • Reptiles • Fish

Fun with FONTS!

- *There are all kinds of managers and leaders*

- **It seems no two have much in common**

- However

- JUST TRY INCONSISTENT FONTS ON ONE SLIDE

- IF YOU AREN'T THAT BRAVE

- **THEN USE DIFFERENT FONTS ON EACH SLIDE**

- **Suddenly, most leaders agree**

- You're Next Eval. might be just as ugly

- ✏️📠📧✂️✏️☺✉!!!!!

You Better Have a Good Reason

- For pulling something like this
- Even if you have this much material—Don't advertise
- Everyone will see it and shut down
- As well they should
- Challenge yourself to use as few slides a possible
- Even challenge the status quo to reduce an old template
- Too much is too much

More from Spencer Beatty...

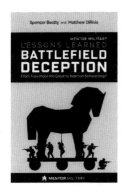

Lessons Learned: Battlefield Deception

A MUST READ for all unit leaders! A quick and insightful compilation of vignettes taken from history. Perfect for educating leaders during professional development sessions. Explore military deception through the venerable lenses of Sun Tzu, Carl von Clausewitz to Norman Schwarzkopf.

These engaging vignettes provide brief but compelling glimpses into the genius and tragedy of wits and wills put to the ultimate test. Learn to incorporate deception into your tactics.

Logistics for the Non Logistician

Logistics is the thing that brings your Soldiers food, water, ammunition, fuel and keeps equipment FMC. Why leave such essentials to someone else, when you never settle for that in any other aspect of being a leader?

· Stay lethal with ammo & fuel expertise.
· Water—turn your Achilles heel into an advantage.
· Improve morale with quality chow
· Contains unique planning sheets for Classes I & III
· Know the key players that affect your combat effectiveness

MDMP: The Military Decision Making Process

Demystify the Military Decision Making Process. Beatty does an excellent job of walking the leader through the steps of MDMP including: Solving the Right Problem, Receipt of Mission, Mission Analysis, Development of COAs, Analyzing COAs, War Gaming, COA Comparison, Approval, and Implementation. There is no other guide on the market that details the MDMP process. The perfect professional development guide for any officer or NCO.

Why Shop from **MentorMilitary.com?**

- Our product selection is curated **specifically for servicemembers**

- **Competitive pricing,** our prices are often lower than Amazon

- Most orders ship within 1 business day

- We ship to **APO/FPOs**

- We offer a 30-Day Money Back guarantee on our books

Visit MentorMilitary.com